What Others are saying...

"This book is a must have for your grants library! This book will allow you to glean the tips from the 'best of the best'. Jana Jane Hexter has done an excellent job of compiling a wealth of invaluable information from the top experts in the grants industry."

-- Gail Vertz, GPC, Chief Executive Officer,
Grant Professionals Association

"A big shout out to Jana for writing a book filled with wisdom and compassion and given to us with a deep spirit of generosity."

-- Jeff Furman, Trustee,
Ben & Jerry's Foundation

"In this thought-provoking book, Jana beautifully expresses the humanity and spirituality of grantwriting. It is not a checklist of steps to follow but a call for deeper relatedness. Jana has a knack for making the interviewees come alive, so in the end it doesn't feel like you've just read a "how-to" book so much as it feels like you have been sitting in a room with this group of fundraising veterans listening to them share their secrets."

-- Lynne Twist, bestselling author of *The Soul of Money*,
Founder and President of the Soul of Money Institute

"The advice is dead-on: for the novice it is eye-opening; for the veteran it is re-enforcing and encouraging. I found my own thoughts, challenges, successes and worries written throughout the book. One thing is for sure: proposal developers need mixed personalities - dominatrix and psychologist, military-grade planner and community healer. It's all here and it's all critical. This is a marvelous gift to proposal writers for our practice, for our institutions, for ourselves."

-- Sarah S. Brophy, author of Is *Your Museum Grant-Ready? Assessing your organization's potential for funding*

"Reading this book was like sitting at the table with the superstars of grant development as they reflect on the nuanced details that have made them successful. The advantage to reading the book, over being at the table, is Jana Hexter's brilliant organization of the anecdotes into a discernible pattern of behavior. Ms. Hexter's own voice is one of story teller-- engaging, humorous, insightful, and personal. Through down-to-earth analogies, practical examples, and a highly personable interpretation of the interviewees' stories, this book presents the key practices of successful grant development in a way that sticks!"

-- Anke Wessels, Executive Director,
Center for Transformative Action

"Grant writing is often a frustrating and difficult exercise. Jana Hexter's book takes an optimistic and slightly spiritual approach to the task of writing good grants while providing the reader with a clear and thorough explanation of the process. She makes grant writing seem almost like fun!"

-- Jane B. O'Connell, President,
Altman Foundation

"I was struck the number of jewels in this book. Most good grant writing books give you the author's expert opinion but Jana's book gives you 25 experts' opinions. She brings out their best thinking as they go beyond the science to the art of good grant writing, something that takes years to master."

-- Michael Wells, GPC, CFRE,
Author of *Grantwriting Beyond the Basics* series

"Jana gives us a fresh perspective on both sides of the development coin by illustrating how fruitful it can be to never see the dividing line between grantor and grantee at all - but see instead the shared goals and human relationships. The whole process of obtaining funding will be so much richer and more productive if we took this approach."

-- Martha Moore, Independent Information Consulting

"This book is the 'Open Sesame' of grant writing's hidden little secrets to successful proposals. Jana Hexter has unlocked the door to show how grant writing is an art form and a science. She reveals the secrets of writing with honesty and integrity. She shares home-spun personal anecdotes and her humor to get the points across and to help us remember them."

--Donald A. Griesmann, ret'd Episcopal clergy and legal services lawyer, virtual volunteer with grant announcements via Twitter (@dgriesmann)

"Grant development is critical to the success of national endeavors in academia, government, and industry. Having access, through this book, to the experience and insights from professional grant developers is priceless. From the first-time proposer to my experienced colleagues that have successfully guided grant development for national centers of research and education, there is information of value in this book. The candid and direct nature of the comments from the grant writers themselves adds a new level of insight and interest in this very useful and readable book."

-- Dr. Kevin D. Franklin, Executive Director, Institute for Computing in Humanities, Arts and Social Science; Senior Research Scientist, National Center for Supercomputing Applications

"Jana Hexter's book provides the keys to the vault for development professionals!"

-- Jim Grant, Communications and Development Director St. Joseph's Addiction Treatment & Recovery Centers

"Candid insights and helpful hints make this book useful for any nonprofit that wants to improve its hit rate in grantwriting. An easy writing style helps the reader learn."

-- Simone P. Joyaux, ACFRE, Joyaux Associates, Author of *Keep Your Donors* and *Strategic Fund Development*

Why This Book is a Gift

The most beautiful experience we can have is the mysterious. It is the fundamental emotion that stands at the cradle of true art and true science. Whoever does not know it and can no longer wonder, no longer marvel, is as good as dead, and his eyes are dimmed.

Albert Einstein

In 2010, I was ready to move into another stage of my career and decided to write a book. I wanted to encapsulate all that I had learned over the years and send it out into the universe — it would be my swan song.

I found a publisher easily and, contract in hand, I started the interviews. They were fascinating, and I learned a lot in each of them. The writing process was surprisingly fun and easy.

Then the publisher broke the contract. Naturally, I was both angry and incredulous. But, I believed that the material was valuable and, with the encouragement of my friends and family, finished it anyway.

Thankfully, around that time I read *The Gift* by Lewis Hyde, and then when I read Charles Eisenstein's *Sacred Economics*, everything clicked into place.

I realized that from the very beginning this book was written in the spirit of gift, and that is how I would publish it.

It has been a labor of love. I've tried to be vulnerable and share myself and what I know as deeply as I can, and I believe the interviewees did the same. It is a creation of my heart, soul, and intellect. I hope that it empowers you and your community.

So, What Do I Mean by Gift? Is That the Same as Free?

Life is a gift. We are each a gift and we are here with gifts to share in the world. If we freely shared our gifts with wise and gracious love within communities of generosity and trust we would be creating the world that our hearts know is possible.

We are used to sale transactions, where we agree that if I give you something you will give me something in return. But a gift is different.

A gift involves reciprocity, going to and fro between a group of people (the root words are re and pro, back and forth). Think about your family or a tribal or religious community. In those circumstances, we give gifts to members of the family not expecting it to be returned to us in the same form. But we know that the gift recipient will give to others when the need arises, and that as a member of that group we will be taken care of. Gifting this book is the same but I am giving it to my global family. It is not an act of charity on my part but more a recognition of our sacred interdependence.

One attribute of gifts is that we like to give them to people who will use and appreciate them and not hoard them. Therefore, I ask that you please use the gift of my book to help our world or pass it along to someone who will do so.

Would you like to take part in an experiment in generosity?

If you would like a copy of the book please email me through my website www.grantwritingrevealed.com and I will send you a discount code for the kindle version and a link to a pdf version. Please use whichever is most convenient for you.

I ask that you keep the gift in flow by reciprocating in whatever way feels right to you, here are some suggestions:

1. Help a neighbor, colleague, friend, or stranger in any way.
2. Do something to cherish the earth.
3. Make a contribution to the charity of your choice.
4. Offer something to me that you would like to give.
5. Another gift that I appreciate is simply spreading the word about my work.

Since we are strangers, I do not have the pleasure of seeing you use my gift or pass it along. So, I invite you to please share your story of how you reciprocated on my website (it can be as short as a few sentences)

www.grantwritingrevealed.com/gift-stories

The creative commons copyright allows you to freely share this book for non-commercial purposes — you can put it on your blog or make photocopies but not sell it or use it to promote advertising. I ask that you also include an attribution any time that you do reproduce it.

Without a blueprint, I'm following my heart in designing this as I go along. So, please visit my website

www.grantwritingrevealed.com for the latest details.

But Why?

There are pioneers in our country who are experimenting with creating more nurturing and sustainable ways of relating. You may have heard of the Karma Kitchen in Berkeley, a restaurant where there are no prices on the menu and where the check reads $0.00 with only this footnote: "*Your meal was a gift from someone who came before you. To keep the chain of gifts alive, we invite you to pay it forward for those dine after you.*" They have served over 30,000 meals. Or, Burning Man which is a gift-based community festival welcoming 48,000+ people.

This is my version of the experiment. It's both idealistic AND practical

The norms in our world are competition, mistrust, scarcity, and survival of the fittest. Our ecological, political, and economic systems are in upheaval and calling for us to evolve and create a new way of relating.

With this leap into the unknown, I am exploring what it is to live my life as a gift and to co-create a gift economy in a global context.

Like everyone else, my deepest yearning is to serve and share my natural gifts and, like everyone else, money often seems an impediment rather than an aid to that. But, something else is possible.

I believe, we are in the formative stages of creating new financial structures that honor our inherent unity. Structures in which money is imbibed with spirit and used in service to our global good rather than as a vehicle of distrust and destruction. Gifting this book is my contribution to creating that structure.

I am committed to the feminine being, powerfully and freely expressed in the world and all life honored as sacred.

Given these beliefs and commitment, I gift this book to you as a step toward the next phase of our evolution in kindness, trust and community.

My deepest wish is that you use this book to sing a song from your soul that benefits us all and 'create the more beautiful world that our hearts know is possible.'[1]

---

[1] Charles Eisenstein's phrase from Sacred Economics.

GRANT WRITING REVEALED

25 EXPERTS SHARE THEIR THEIR ART, SCIENCE, AND SECRETS

by

Jana Jane Hexter

www.grantschampion.com

Published by
Grantomatics LLC
P.O. Box 764
Trumansburg, NY 14886
www.grantschampion.com

Cover Design by Amelia Wise

Copyediting by Melissa Brown & Associates LLC and Ann Redelfs.

Library of Congress Cataloging-in-Publication Data

ISBN-13:
978-1477613108

ISBN-10:
1477613102

To my parents, for being born to you was the first of many blessings in my life.
I love you.

Disclaimer

This book designed to provide information on developing grant proposals. It is given with the understanding that the publisher and author are not engaged in rendering legal, accounting or other professional services. If legal advice is required, the services of a competent professional should be sought.

The purpose of this book is to educate and entertain. The author and publisher shall have neither liability nor responsibility to any person or entity with respect to any loss or damage caused, directly or indirectly, by the information contained in this book.

If you do not wish to be bound by this the above, you may return this book for a full refund.

Contents

PROGRAM AND PROJECT DESIGN

MAKING A CASE AND WRITING THE
APPLICATION

THE SECRETS

The Big Picture

Heart-Centered Grant Development

Acknowledgements

This book wouldn't have been possible without the generosity of the people who took the time to reflect on their work and methods and then share that with me, a total stranger to many of you. Thank you.

My children, for your unbridled enthusiasm, space and time to write, and your absolute faith that Mum was producing something worthy of the sacrifice. Iain for being you. Doug for encouraging me in this business and for giving me the financial cushion to write this. Maren for being such a loving presence in the world.

David Allee, the most wonderful boss that anyone could hope for, who encouraged me to spread my wings and take a grant writing class. Hope you're having as much fun up there. Paula Peter, thank you for your wisdom and always pointing me in the right direction. Kari Willis for your insight. Tori Wishart, Melissa, Emma, Ken, and Ann for your eagle-eyed editing.

Jennifer Berezan, David Darling, Deuter, and Deva Premal for your beautiful music that kept me going through many long hours of writing. I hope this book includes a touch of the ethereal beauty that comes through your music.

My friends Susan Anton, Jalaja Bonheim, Cara Eve, Damaris Vasquez, Daphne Cohn, Sarah Craft, Ryan Fix, Gina Inzinna, JaiHari Meyerhoff, Christin Munsch, Pam Moss, Kelly Patwell, Sue Sandritter, Bert Scholl, Carl Sinclair, and Dan Tillemans: with deep gratitude for your love, humor, and support. I treasure you.

The Friars of the Atonement for showing me what it means to live committed to loving service.

To the source of all life, thank you for the grace of this one.

Introduction

Imagine sitting down in a room with 25 people who collectively raised $1.7 billion dollars during their careers, with 400 years of combined writing experience on more than 24,000 grant proposals.

What would you want to know? Their secrets to success, what makes them tick? The things they absolutely avoid doing? Me too.

That's why I interviewed 25 people considered "top" grant developers and asked them to reflect on what they do and how they do it. Here, I share with you what I learned. I was touched by their generosity of spirit in sharing decades of experience so freely and hope that you will be too.

I invite you to savor their words, drink in their wisdom, and use it to raise more money for your organization.

Who are Top Grant Developers?

As I set out to interview 'top grant developers' I first had to define what that meant. I chose three criteria for the selection process:

Successful track record. The top grant developers I interviewed have raised an average of $67 million each during their careers.

After looking at the dollar amounts raised, defining 'successful track record' can get sticky, especially for people who work on staff and often have to submit proposals that they know won't get funded because their board or boss insists.

Not surprisingly, the average success rate for staff was 66% compared to 79% for consultants. You may think that I would have chosen people whose success rate was above 90%, but experience tells me that when someone's success rate is that high, they are cherry picking assignments or staying with the tried and true and not encouraging their organization to expand its boundaries.

For example, Frank Mandley raised over half a billion dollars in his career with a large school district and yet his team's success rate was consistently between 58% and 63%.

This tells me that they were stretching them-

Top <u>Foundation</u> Grant Developer Profile
$19 million raised
17 years experience
965 grants developed

Top <u>Government</u> Grant Developer Profile
$154 million raised
20 years experience
1,017 grants developed

selves and applying for new programs—and it is also indicative of the fact that regardless of how beautifully something is planned and presented, sometimes it just doesn't win for reasons beyond your control.

Significant experience. The people I interviewed have an average of 18 years of experience as grant developers and written an average of 984 grants. There is an even mix of foundation and government grant developers as well geographic and gender distribution.

Their experience ranges from the performing arts, K-12 education, housing, health care, science and technology, women's development, museums, and hunger.

Three had worked at foundations and shared what they learned from being on the other side of the fence.

A strong reputation among their peers or funders. I located them through my network at the Grant Professionals Association and Association of Fundraising Professionals. I also called several foundation contacts and asked them who they thought were their best grantees.

There are many grant developers who meet these criteria, and I don't claim to have interviewed them all. I say just that the people I interviewed are truly experts in the field. I did not include authors of other grant development books because I want to ensure fresh perspectives.

So, What's Their Secret?

When I set out to write this book, I was determined not to write a Grant Writing 101 book. I've been in the business for 15 years and raised more than $28 million. In the interviews, I listened from this perspective and gently probed for what lay below the surface. I thought that by finding out what made people tick I would learn the secret to their success. I learned something new in every interview and had lots of 'aha' moments. All of those nuggets are included in the book.

After doing the interviews I sat down to read through my notes. After some time, they all started melding into one another, and it almost seemed as if I had interviewed one person because their similarities were so strong. Actually, it was more like two people because foundation grant developers and government grant developers are slightly different beasts.

> **Their Secret Is.....**
>
> Top grant developers don't do one, two, or five things that you don't do. Their secret is that they have a holistic approach and consistently apply the 24 essential elements of grant development to succeed. These elements are described in detail in this book.

For a break, I picked up Jared Diamond's <u>Guns, Germs, and Steel</u> and opened it at the section where he describes the Anna Karenina Principle. He quotes the first line of Anna Karenina:

> 'Happy families are all alike; every unhappy family is unhappy in its own way.'

> By that sentence, Tolstoy meant that, in order to be happy a marriage must succeed in many different

respects; sexual attraction, agreement about money, child discipline, religion, in-laws, and other vital issues. Failure in any one of those essential respects can doom a marriage even if it has all the other ingredients needed for happiness. The principle can be extended to understanding much else about life besides marriage.

We tend to seek easy, single-factor explanations of success. For most things, though, success actually requires avoiding many separate possible causes of failure.

The Anna Karenina Principle holds true for grant development. Top grant developers' secret to success is that they <u>consistently</u> do ALL of the things they need to succeed and therefore, as Jared Diamond suggests, avoid several possible causes of failure.

For a moment, imagine that you are a master builder. You know that to build a house you need an architect, electrician, plumber, and roofer. You need to make sure that you choose a sound piece of land, plan carefully, and build a solid foundation before you start construction. You'd also need to finish the space and decorate it so that it felt like home.

Miss any one of these essential steps and your home would either be uninhabitable or uncomfortable.

Grant development is the same. If you don't attend to the 24 essential elements described in the chapters of this book, your grant won't be funded, or if it is, you'll live to regret it. That may be disheartening news if you're skimming this book looking for the single alchemical secret to winning grants.

But, if you're interested in looking at what you do and how you do it with an eye to improving, then you're in the right spot. We're going to look at those 24 elements, and I invite you to look for your weak spots and put actions in place to address them.

But being able to construct a sound house does not make a master builder. For masters, the basics of building are so ingrained they manage the process and avoid foreseeable pitfalls. When that happens, there's space for artistry to emerge.

Top grant developers have internalized grant development essentials so that they consistently do the essential steps, leaving space for the magical 24th element to emerge — the artistry.

Know Thyself

We all know that if you want to improve anything, you need to realistically assess where you are now. So, if you want to be a more successful grant developer, it's useful to look at where your current strengths and weaknesses lie.

We'll look at each of the 24 elements of success, and you'll hear from the top grant developers about how or why they focus on them and what it looks like when you put grant development theory into practice.

As you read, I invite you to ask, "Do I have that skill?" I'm sure that you'll be pleasantly surprised. The next question is "Do I consistently apply it?" If you don't, reflect on why.

Be gentle with yourself; don't use it as an excuse to admonish yourself for one more thing you don't do. This is a chance to simply look and see if there are a couple of key things that you skip when it comes to grants, either because you underestimate their importance or don't like doing them.

Once you see where the missing links in your chain are, you might just decide to fill in the blanks. Or, you might realize that you avoid them because you're really not good at them. In that case, team up with someone with that strength who can fill the missing link.

Consistently apply and focus on all 24 elements either as an individual or as part of a team, and you'll increase both your success and enjoyment of the grant development process.

I believe that grant development can be fun, fulfilling, and empowering for you and your organization. My intention is that this book helps you discover or rediscover that for yourself and simultaneously spurs you into action that propels your organization forward and benefits our communities.

A Note About Terminology: The Grant Professionals Association doesn't use the term grantwriting because it puts all of the focus on writing when, in fact, success lies in the accumulation of many other skills such as strategic planning, organizational development, interpersonal and team leadership skills, and research acumen.

I use the term grant development—for that is indeed what we do, develop a plan of action, write it cogently, and then submit it to the right funder at the right time based on our research and knowledge of their interests.

The Grant Professional Certification Competencies: The only psychometrically proven test of grant development skill available is the Grant Professional Certification Institute (GPCI).

The test is based on 61 grant development competencies and skills. In this book, I relate some of the chapters to the competencies.

My intention is not to describe each and every competency but to put several of them into a real-world context and explain how some very accomplished grant developers have applied these concepts over the years.

The Grant Experts
Interviewed

Jonathan Bank is the Artistic Director of the Mint Theater Company in New York City. minttheater.org

Alice Boyd is the Managing Partner of Bailey Boyd Associates, Inc., founded in 1989. Specializing in community development, and municipal funding, Bailey Boyd Associates has secured in excess of $130 million and has one of the strongest records for grant writing and administration in Massachusetts. www.baileyboyd.com

Melissa S. Brown teaches successful proposal writing for The Fund Raising School and at Indiana University. She researched and wrote *Giving USA* from 2001 through 2010 and is now a consultant advising nonprofits about fundraising and findings from research about charitable giving. www.MelissaSBrownAssociates.com

Linda Gatten Butler, MSW, ACSW, LISW-S, is the Founder and Past President of the Miami Valley Ohio Chapter of GPA, a national GPA Board member, and a Licensed Independent Social Worker Supervisor. She has offered grant seeking, fundraising, training and managing for over 180 organizations since 1994. www.Butler-Consulting.com

Susan Caruso Green, GPC, is President of the Resource Development Network, LLC. She is the former Contributions Coordinator for Citi's retail banking system, President of the Cranford Fund for Educational Excellence and membership chair of the Grant Professionals Assoc.- NJ Chapter. http://www.ResourceDevelopmentNetwork.com

Mark Eiduson is Senior Program Officer at The Roddenberry Foundation but at the time of the interview was Director of Strategic Partnerships at the Flintridge Center. He has worked in the nonprofit and foundation sector for 20 years, enjoying the proposal-writing process from both sides of the desk.
www.roddenberryfoundation.org

Diane Gedeon-Martin is President of The Write Source. Since 1993 she has worked with more than 240 nonprofit organizations in 25 states and Washington, DC to help them achieve their goals through grant proposals she prepared ranging from $5,000 to $5 million. She has taught at The Fund Raising School at Indiana University since 2001.
www.write-source.com

John Hicks, CFRE is President and CEO of JC Geever, Inc.. Over a career of 25 years, John has helped nonprofits build and grow foundation and corporate grant-seeking programs. John is a speaker and author for The Foundation Center and is a member of the faculty of Columbia University's Master's Program in Fundraising Management.
www.jcgeever.com

Mary Knepper is the Grants Manager at St. Joseph's Hospital Health Center, Syracuse, NY. She has more than $25 million in approved grants. Her prior experience includes performing arts and music education.
www.sjhsyr.org

Marianne Lockwood is the Co-founder and President Emeritus of the Orchestra of St. Luke's and DiMenna Center for Classical Music. She has overseen St. Luke's growth from a modest chamber ensemble into the foremost chamber orchestra in the country. Her culminating act at St. Luke's was a successful $37 million capital campaign.

Frank Mandley, is CEO and President of F. Mandley & Associates, Inc. For more than 20 years, he served as Grants Administration and Government Programs Director for the Broward County Schools, the sixth largest public school system in the country. During his tenure the school district raised over $524 million in competitive grants. www.fmandleyassociates.com

Diane Nicholson began writing grant proposals when she worked as a program director for a nonprofit org-anization that was under-funded and over-committed. Her grant development business focuses on helping small nonprofit organizations tell their story in a compelling manner.

Mariann Payne is Director of Advancement, Woodstock Theological Center. She has been working in advancement for 14 years with an emphasis on education, research, and faith-based initiatives. http://woodstock.georgetown.edu

Dory Rand is President of Woodstock Institute, a leading nonprofit research and policy organization focused on fair lending, wealth creation, and financial systems reform nationally and in Chicago. www.woodstockinst.org

Ann Redelfs is CEO of Redelfs LLC. Ann has developed successful grants for more than 30 years for universities, national research centers, and nonprofit organizations. She has worked at several national centers that focus on supporting the nation's scientists in their research and educational endeavors. Ann at Redelfs dot us

Johna Rodgers, GPC, is a Grant Writer for the Green River Regional Educational Cooperative, a consortium of 36 school districts in Kentucky. A problem-solver by nature with a toolbox that includes program development and management, as well as writing, thinking, training and facilitation, she has developed $40+ million in grants over 10 years. www.grrec.ky.gov

Tony Silbert is President of Silbert Consulting Services, Inc. Since 1996, he has been a consultant focusing on grant development, research, strategy, and evaluation for organizations of all sizes, covering virtually every aspect of the "nonprofit" world. www.silbertconsulting.com

Bill Smith, GPC, is Senior Director of Corporate Relations, Second Harvest Food Bank of Middle Tennessee, where he tripled grant production in five years. Bill has served as President of the national Grant Professionals Association. He specializes in corporate and foundation grants and mentored new grant professionals who are finding great success in the field. http://www.billofwrites.com

Caitlin Stanton has more than a decade of fundraising and program experience in global philanthropy for social change and women's rights. She is currently based in the San Francisco Bay Area, where she balances work with the Global Fund for Women with raising her twin boys. http://www.globalfundforwomen.org/

Alan Tiano, GPC is the Senior Grant Specialist for Broward County, Florida. He has 16 years of experience in the field. Formerly the Chief Operating Officer of Hispanic Unity of Florida, he is a long-time activist for people living with AIDS, women's rights, gay rights, and the lives of immigrants and refugees.

Dr. Bernard Turner, GPC, has more than 23 years of diversified experience in the grants profession. His experience includes grant development, training, managing, and reviewing for local, state, federal, and private funding sources. He is a trainer/consultant for the Center for Nonprofit Management in Nashville, TN. www.btconsult.org

John White is part of the team establishing the Aquaculture Stewardship Council. At the time of the interview he was Director for Development at the Marine Stewardship Council. During his four years in charge of fundraising at the MSC, income raised by the small fundraising team more than doubled, including significant multi-year and unrestricted major grants. www.asc-aqua.org

Nancy L. Withbroe, CFRE, serves as Senior Director, Development of Share Our Strength, a national nonprofit based in Washington, DC. She has worked with organizations for more than 20 years, raising more than $17 million to date in grants and other charitable gifts from individual and institutional donors. www.nokidhungry.org.

Gail Widner, PhD, GPC, owner of Business Communications Consulting, served as manager of the Grants Program with the South Carolina Department of Education for nine years, during which time she worked on nearly $1 billion in federal grants and assistance programs.

Marilyn Zlotnik, GPC, is Vice President for Development and Communications at Metis Associates. She has collaborated with school systems, institutions of higher education, state agencies, and non-profits to raise more than $250 million to improve the lives of children and families. www.metisassociates.com

RESEARCHING
PROSPECTS

Element 1

Three Core Beliefs About Prospect Research

Illustrates GPCI Competencies

1.03. Identify methods of locating funding sources.

1.04. Identify techniques to learn about specific funders.

1.05. Identify methods for maintaining, tracking, and updating information on potential funders.

Remember your first crush in school? I'm willing to bet that you didn't spot them in the hallway, stroll right up and ask them on a date.

Oh, no. You found out who they were, where they lived, who they hung out with, who their sister hung out with, where they walked their dog, what their favorite color was, and what music they liked etc. etc. *ad infinitum*.

Until, finally, after weeks of planning you figured out the best approach and plucked up the courage to ask them out.

Top grant developers are like hormonal teenagers when it comes to prospect research. They know that it's foundational and fundamental and that putting time and effort into research early on can make the difference between winning and losing down the road. They thoroughly research each and every prospect. They know that winning takes lots of time and effort in the form of relationship building, planning, and writing so they'll only proceed when they have built a solid foundation of research.

John White is a thoroughly charming former British diplomat turned Development Director at the Marine Stewardship Council, and he clearly makes this point.

> Time spent on research is never wasted. I suppose you could reach a stage where research doesn't lead anywhere in the short term but if you keep good records and don't waste research then you won't waste time down the line.

Other books outline how do to prospect research, but here I want to convey the field's top players' attitude to research that is founded on three beliefs.

Belief 1: There's Gold in Dem Der Hills

Common wisdom is that foundations are like Avalon, shrouded behind mists that only a few select people can pierce. But top grant developers, such as John Hicks, a New York-based consultant, see them as clearly visible to all who care to look.

> If you think about it we do have access to a lot of data about foundations, and if you spend time looking at that data you can begin to at least get a sense of the foundation's corporate culture and values by looking at what they say about themselves and at their 990-PF or other public records to see who they are supporting. You are not able to do this with individual donors. Which ten charities did Donald Trump personally support last year? I don't know that because I don't have access to Mr. Trump's tax return.

John's outlook is one of sufficiency rather than scarcity. He expects to find enough background data about foundations to help him decide whether to proceed and he undertakes his exploration within that context.

Belief 2: Research Saves Time

Even if we know that something is abundant we don't usually seek it out unless we value it. Foundations are human-centered organizations and top grant developers know that it saves time if you find out as much as possible about the people at the foundation and their intentions.

We are the kind of people who understand the adage "luck frequents the prepared mind." We don't leave things to chance although, as we'll see later, we know the magic of serendipity.

> Grant development isn't about the writing but a process of developing a mutual understanding of your common point of interest with a funder; prospect research is the first step in the process.

Marianne Lockwood is a one-woman whirlwind that founded what has become New York's most eclectic orchestral group—the Orchestra of St. Luke's. She is engaging and witty but under her free-spirited irreverence lies a determined focus.

> I have an aversion to the cold call, to the mass mailing of proposals to just anybody because it happens to say in a line in their guidelines that they support the arts. When you haven't done your homework, it wastes your time and wastes their time. You tend to antagonize them as much as anything else... It comes down to doing your homework.

I know that we're all busy and it's tempting to get to the writing as soon as possible, but Marianne beautifully illustrates that if you don't do enough research you'll a) waste your time, and b) irritate people.

Neither of those options are a recipe for success so I err on the side of doing too much homework. It's human nature to ignore things that we don't like and in grant development we often ignore what foundations say.

We want them to fund orphanages in Nepal when they quite explicitly say that they fund orphanages in Thailand. But they can't be all things to all people. Top grant developers know that they can save themselves a lot of time by accepting what foundations do fund <u>and</u> what they don't fund.

Belief 3: It's Worth Searching for Your Mutual Interests

A point that you'll hear many times in this book is that winning grants isn't about the writing. It's a process of developing a mutual understanding of your common points of interest with a funder. Prospect research is the first step in the process.

Top grant developers will spend days, weeks, and months learning about funders so that they can begin to see where their points of interest interconnect.

One way to learn about foundation prospects is through Meet the Funder sessions. Tony Silbert lives in Los Angeles so he knows all about congestion and is spot on when he described these sessions as a zoo. But top grant developers will *always* go to Meet the Funder sessions, and Nancy Withbroe explained why.

> You are hearing directly from the people themselves, what is important to them and the institution they

represent. There is only so much you can learn from databases and the information is often out-of-date, as it is based on the 990s or other published sources of information on funding.

Even their websites—by the time something is uploaded onto the website as a new strategic plan or a new direction, it has probably been in the works for years, and you are not going to know that unless you get out the door, get to know them, meet with them, and go to sessions where they are presenting…anything that you can do to get to know the people and to get inside their heads will serve you very well.

Questions to Consider

1. Do I love spending hours doing background research and finding every last shred of information or do I stop at 60% and call it adequate by choice or necessity?
2. If you're a 60% person, maybe you're just not a person who relishes detective work and details or you simply don't have the time. If that's the case, it's not the end of the world. You could find a colleague who enjoys that kind of probing or has the time to do it and ask for their help.
3. After reading this chapter, can I reframe background research as a necessary component of grants success and do it as thoroughly as I can?
4. Do I make "Meet the Funder" sessions, foundation and government webinars, or other opportunities to hear directly from program officers a priority?

---○---

A Story: When Research Pays Off

Years ago, we won a $100,000 grant from the Tony Randall Theatrical Fund in their first year of open competition. The fund was administered by Tony's widow, Heather, and a panel of people that she gathered to review proposals.

Apparently, I don't know if I was the only one, or one of very few people, who actually bothered to do any research about what was important to Tony and talk about that in the proposal.

Everybody described their projects, and I described my project, as well, but I spent more time trying to get a grip on how to talk to them specifically in a way that I thought would be meaningful. Not just a compelling project but a project that I thought Tony would like….

Maybe I am a little better suited to thinking about who the audience is than some others because I have an audience every night. I am sure that every grant developer is thinking about who is reading, or I hope everyone is, but I have much more experience with audience feedback than most grant developers have because I stand in the lobby every night when we do a show.

Jonathan Bank, The Mint Theater, New York

---○---

Element 2

Knowing When to Respond to a Request for Proposals

Illustrates GPCI Competencies

1.08. *Determine best matches between funders and specific programs.*

1.09. *Interpret grant application request for proposal (RFP) guidelines and requirements to accurately assess funder intent.*

2.07. *Identify strategies and procedures for obtaining internal institutional support and approval of decision-makers for grant-seeking activities.*

Creating a government or large foundation proposal is always a herculean task — even for those of us who have been doing it for years on a full-time basis.

But, usually we have to make quick decisions about whether to go for it or let it slide. That's not easy when there is a lot of money at stake and it takes skill and experience to know when to bite.

Top grant developers shared three strategies that they use to help them make fast decisions: a) deciding if they *want* to win the grant, b) teaching their team to be selective, and c) being willing to walk away.

Do You Want To Win?

While our initial response to the question of whether we want to win is a blindingly obvious, "of course we do," the people I interviewed are more circumspect.

There are grants that we can win but it would take a program in a direction that doesn't align with the organization's priorities. Many of us have experienced mission creep and seen organizations damaged by taking on grants that just weren't right for them.

Therefore, we make sure that the grant will serve the organization rather than the other way around. John White summarized this beautifully when he described how his team analyzes grant opportunities.

> We think hard within the organization as to what the funder is saying they are interested in is also something that part of our work fits. Sometimes you can see the fit very easily.

> Sometimes you would be distorting things so much that it is simply not worth it in a sense you could end up either getting money for a low-priority activity or in some cases ending up making an argument that really isn't sustainable.

> I think it is a question of just looking, interpreting, reading, and understanding what funders are about and try to get inside their heads and think what makes them tick.

> What are the things they want to do? What are they trying to achieve and do you fit the bill? If you don't, frankly it's not worth your time or theirs in following up a response.

Help Your Team Be Selective Using the Glove Approach

When deliberating about whether to put time into a Request for Proposals (RFP) consider some of the more esoteric factors in addition to the obvious ones:

- What time of year is it? December, July, and August are half as productive as other months.
- Will your CEO make this RFP an organizational priority so that you can get people to give their time and energy?
- What's your team's capacity? Are they familiar with the funding agency and can step right in, or will they need a lot of handholding?
- What stage is the program idea? Do you have a well-conceived plan and just need to fill in some blanks and write it up, or do you have the seed of an idea and need plenty of time for strategizing and thinking it through?

Once you're clear about all the factors to consider, Frank Mandley has a wonderful suggestion about how to help your team make the decision to move ahead.

> Say to them "Here is the RFP, which is a glove, and here are your needs, which is a hand. Can we at least get four of the fingers into the glove or is this a fit for only one thumb? Because if that's the case then we shouldn't do it.

I like Frank's analogy because it really points out that a poorly fitting grant will be an ongoing annoyance rather than a temporary inconvenience, just like clothes that don't fit. And, grants are definitely gloves not mittens. People want to see them as mittens into which they can slide just about everything, but that just isn't the case.

When They Want You to Apply for Everything

You know the scenario: your agency is short of money and your board or boss is pushing you to apply for as much as possible as often as possible. This scatter shot approach isn't effective but it's difficult to convince them otherwise.

In grants, you fare better when you put a lot of energy into a few good prospects. Frank Mandley worked in a very large organization, and he told me that after about five years they began to trust his judgment rather than ask his team to apply for every competition in sight.

How did that turnaround come about? Surprisingly, from their success in winning two grants they were told to write without working closely with the program team.

> The poor departments that took the grants on couldn't live with what we wrote because we didn't know what we were writing about. I mean we knew what the RFP was and we were smart enough to respond to the RFP. One was a five-year grant and they spent the first three years amending the thing a million times because they couldn't live with how we had written it in total isolation.

The adage "the worse you want it, the worse you get it" applies to grants. While such disasters could have tarnished his team's reputation, Frank used them to educate his leadership by saying, "This really doesn't work when you tell us to do this stuff without the help of people who will be implementing the project. You create more problems than you solve."

When they applied for fewer grants in a more targeted way, they raised more money. Being direct pays off in the long run even if people are initially disappointed by an opportunity forgone.

If your boss asks you to apply for everything, consider asking colleagues about their *"wish we'd never gotten it funded"* horror story (most experienced grant developers have them).

Then share those stories with your team and illustrate that a thoughtful glove-fitting approach that considers all of an RFP's pros and cons will work better than the mitten approach.

> **CORE BELIEFS OF TOP GRANT DEVELOPERS**
>
> **Belief 1:** There are plenty of fish in the sea – if we miss this one another will swim by.
>
> **Belief 2:** We must have the right programmatic bait.
>
> **Belief 3:** I'm skilled and when I use my time wisely I can win.
>
> **Belief 4:** Time is precious and there is no point wasting my talents on something that won't yield results.

Don't Be Afraid to Walk Away

Melissa Brown, past Editor of *Giving USA*, said, "Don't be afraid to walk away. Make sure that you match your mission with the funder's. If the match isn't there, learn to say 'No, this isn't a fit' and move on to another opportunity." This attitude is rooted in self-confidence that manifests in several beliefs highlighted in the box on the last page.

When you're not confident that there are other options out there and unsure of your skill in securing grants you're more likely to grasp at whatever walks by. It really helps if you can take a deep breath and be selective regardless of how much your organization needs funding.

Questions to Consider

1. Are you and your team confident enough to walk away?
2. If not, take another look at the beliefs above. What are your thoughts/beliefs about grant seeking? Try to be as honest as possible about this. Look at those thoughts that flit through your mind as you think about applying for a big grant—this is just an exercise. Then consider using Byron Katie's inquiry process "The Work" to question those beliefs.
   - Is it true?
   - Can you absolutely know that it's true?
   - How do you react, what happens, when you believe that thought?
   - Who would you be without the thought?

   Byron Katie has lots of other resources on her website designed to help you recognize and question underlying beliefs (http://thework.com).
3. Can you objectively help your team assess the fit between the RFP and the project?

If you would like to further develop this skill there are lots of high-quality articles about reading RFPs on the Internet, including sites such as charitychannel.com and proposalwriter.com.

BUILDING
RELATIONSHIPS

Element 3

Know Each Person's Role and Responsibility in Foundations

Illustrates GPCI Competencies

8.2. Identify strategies to determine funder-relation approaches that suit fund-seeking entities' missions, cultures, and values.

You wouldn't walk into a restaurant and ask the chef to wait on you or expect the waitress to cook your food.

In all organizations, people have their own jobs and spheres of responsibility. Top grant developers know what roles people play in foundations and use that information to develop stronger relationships with their funders.

Nancy Withbroe is an elegant woman who exudes inner calm and works at Share Our Strength in Washington DC. She explained this to me in a way that really sunk in.

> Remember that the relationships are really at the core of foundation grant seeking as much as any other forms of fundraising. And being true to those relationships and understanding the roles that the different people play in the foundation and respecting those roles, even as you are trying to find the person you can connect with, is really critical and often overlooked.

Let's look at the roles of the three main players in foundations — gatekeepers, program officers, and trustees.

Gatekeepers Open Doors

Marianne Lockwood of the Orchestra of St. Luke's and Mariann Payne of the Woodstock Theological Center at Georgetown University are certifiably charming.

I sense that both of them totally and utterly love building relationships, and they shared how they do it. First of all, they intentionally get to know the gatekeepers as Marianne Lockwood explained.

> I always make an effort to include program officers' assistants because it often helps getting somebody to take your phone calls... Sometimes, they hold the keys and if you can get them to be sympathetic they also have a way of opening doors. I am always very conscious of making sure that everybody I am in contact with, I have a good relationship with.

Mariann Payne lost no time in charming me from the start of our interview, and so when we got to the questions about relationship building I knew I was in for some juicy stuff. She didn't disappoint. For those of us who feel tongue-tied in these situations, she even gave us a script.

> I tend to call the gatekeeper and schmooze them until I get a sense of who is the right person for me to reach out to. I say, "Well on your website you say these are the four program officers in X. I am trying to have a conversation with one of them about what we do and which one of them is kind of interested in Y?" So I kind of work the gatekeeper a little.

She continued to tell me what she does once she gets a meeting.

> I take the gatekeeper a gift, usually a book. So, when I walk in I say, "I would really like an opportunity to meet Suzy because she was so helpful in setting up

this meeting," and so the Director will take me over to meet Suzy, the gatekeeper, and I look her in the eye and say "Thank you, I just brought you a little something."

I got the sense from both women that while they are consciously turning on the charm faucet they genuinely love getting to know new people. For them it's fun and rewarding and because of their sincerity it lands well for the recipient.

Program Officers Listen, Advise, and Persuade

Program officers are like talent scouts for major league teams. Top grant developers know that the program officer's primary job is to find good projects to fund, as John Hicks pointed out.

> My observation is that foundations are entrepreneurial institutions that happen in many cases to have staff and boards who are risk-averse. In most cases a grant is never put in front of a board...unless the staff member of the foundation feels that it is a good investment. They don't get paid to bring bad investments before boards.

But while program officers are responsible for scouting out good projects, they are not omnipotent, as Mark Eiduson pointed out. Mark spent years as a program officer in a Los Angeles foundation.

> They do not generally have the authority to green light your grant request. Program officers can say no, but they can't usually say yes. That's usually the trustees' job. And no matter how well you are liked or loved as a potential grantee, the trustees' decision-

making process does not incorporate that relationship.

But the question that we all grapple with is "How close a relationship do you need in order for a program officer to put your project before their board?" Mark Eiduson surprised me when he said,

> You don't have to be best friends with a program officer. In fact, program officers don't have time to be everybody's best friend. If you feel comfortable enough just picking up the phone and calling and saying "Can we apply? Here is an exciting project that appears to fit with your guidelines. I have read it online. I just want to run it past you."

> If you feel comfortable enough to do that, you have a strong enough relationship with the program officer.

> As a program officer I can't know everything that is happening in the field if we have multiple fields in which we fund. It is really helpful to me to feel comfortable enough to say, "Hey, what is the latest development in gang violence intervention? What is happening in the city, community, state, the nation? What do I need to know?"

> So if I can call you as an expert on one of these topics and you feel comfortable enough to call me and say can we apply for X, we have a great relationship. It is the perfect working relationship.

> That way also you don't get freaked out if you don't know anybody at the foundation. And you don't have to face, how do I make this woman my best friend to send in a Letter of Interest (LOI).

Now, this is counter to the popular wisdom that you should build as strong a relationship as possible with program officers.

I've thought about his comment for months, and I think that it's deceptively simple. While Mark says that you just need to have the kind of relationship where you can ask about what's going on, in reality, it takes a lot for most of us to call someone up and tell them that you don't know something. While it doesn't have to be a personal friendship, I assert that there is deep undercurrent of trust and respect that needs to exist for such candor.

Tony Silbert, a consultant in Los Angeles, had a similar, no-nonsense response.

> The only reason I use the contacts is really just to get the lay of the land and the timing and the mood of the place but it's not like, at least for me as a consultant, my interaction is going to affect the outcome.
>
> It just sort of tells us what we are up against, and if it is even worth applying. Not having connections doesn't mean anything to me.
>
> At this point with the foundations that I have relationships with, and I know someone mostly at all the major ones here in L.A., it is very much like, "Hey here's what I've got today, what do you think?"

On the face of it, it also sounds like Tony doesn't think of these relationships as particularly strong but if I called program officers at the top Los Angeles foundations tomorrow, I doubt that more than one would call me back within two weeks.

I think Tony underestimates the depth of his existing relationships, and when he calls up and asks, "What do you think of X or Y," he is taking the first step in the negotiation dance that surrounds all grants.

> "I think grant making has changed in twenty years so that getting a grant from a foundation has become more and more a process of negotiation. So letting it solely rest with a proposal I don't think is a good idea. I think you have to understand there's going to be a relationship building process."
>
> John Hicks
> J.C. Geever Inc.

Trustees Decide

If program officers can't green light a project then grant developers are left with two options: either build a relationship with a board member or empower the program officer to advocate for you in the board room. We'll talk about the latter option in Element 5.

If you're focusing on building relationships with trustees you need to be mindful of the organization's internal politics as Nancy Withbroe learned.

Even if you have a connection with a board member, don't go around the staff unless it is a family foundation where they don't have any staff or the staff is merely someone doing the paperwork and not a professional administrator.

They are hired to manage the process and manage the relationships, and if you go around them to a board member without letting the staff know that you are doing that, it can really poison the relationship with the staff member that you are going to be working with on a regular basis going forward.

I'm leery of telling the program officer that I'm planning on contacting a board member in case the program officer puts a quash on it, but Nancy points out, "Some board members may resent being approached if they perceive that you are trying to go around the staff. Full disclosure of all relationships usually works best—letting staff know if you are also reaching out to board members, and vice versa—so that they know you are following the 'rules' but also have deep connections among multiple decision makers."

Interacting with foundation trustees is often different from program officers. As wealthy and/or retired individuals they often don't have 9-5 jobs and are more open to social events than program officers.

And, as Nancy Withbroe mentioned, "Trustees tend to have more of an emotional and visceral kind of feeling about their foundation's work." Given that she suggests two ways of developing stronger relationships with them.

Help them feel good by having handwritten notes go out from the clientele to them or inviting them to events where they get to interact with the people you are serving. Those kinds of things that really help them get that charge about what you are doing. Some of them are also interested in the actual issues and may want to be part of a more substantive conversation along the way.

Knowing who is responsible for what can save you from misjudging authority, offending anyone, or wasting their time and yours. Once you've identified the person responsible for decision-making, the next step in the process is taking the time to understand their concerns and interests and see how you can advance them.

Questions to Consider

1. In what ways can I cultivate relationships with trustees differently from program officers?
2. How can I thank gatekeepers who have helped us?

> Success comes from "checking where the decision is being made and talking to those people."
> Caitlin Stanton
> Global Fund for Women

Element 4

Getting Through the Door

Illustrates GPCI Competency

8.4. Identify methods of relationship cultivation, communication, recognition, and stewardship that might appeal to specific funders.

Most grant development books blithely tell you to make contact with the foundation and talk to the program officer. But in reality that's easier said than done.

The dirty truth about this work is that it can take months and even years of attempts to build a relationship with a trustee or program officer before your effort pays off.

But top grant developers know that it makes a huge difference and so are willing to put the time and effort into the cultivation process. Marianne Lockwood is simply masterful in her ability to build relationships with people and she put her finger on the issue.

> People giving to people: to me that is absolutely critical. If you can get to an institution and actually get in the door and talk to somebody, you are three quarters of the way there. It makes all the difference in the world when they have a chance to see the face of the person who is representing the organization and get a sense that you are not just words on a piece of paper. I think it creates a certain amount of trust that really helps when you are trying to make your case.

All of the most successful grants that I have gotten have been because I have managed to meet and talk. You can just make your case in a completely different way when you are face to face with somebody. You can get close on the phone, but it is just not the same thing as being there in person. But of course that is the big challenge, getting in.

So, what tactics do top grant developers use to get through the door?

Informational Interviews

Asking for an inform-ational about the foundation sometimes works as a conversation starter, but as Marianne Lockwood points out this strategy is much harder with large pro-fessional foundations "be-cause they don't have the time or they see right through and know what you are really trying to do is come and ask for money."

Six Conversation Starters

1. Informational Interviews
2. Ask for an Introduction
3. Cold Calls
4. Ask for Advice
5. Cultivation Events
6. Letters of Interest

Ask for an Introduction

As with all things in life, success begets success. Top grant developers ask their existing foundation contacts to introduce them to new foundations as John White explained.

We've had a number of cases where we've identified a possible source of funding, not had any contact but have said to a program officer who knows us well, "Do you know anybody at X?" and they say - "Oh yes, I used to work with him at such and such a foundation and I will drop him a note." So quite often that works and once you have made that first contact it's a heck of a lot easier.

Cold Calling

Cold calling sometimes works, and Mariann Payne has a good track record with them. She starts with a letter or email describing the initiative and that she would like to visit to share a strategic new program and to learn about what they're working on. When she calls, she asks

"Could we have coffee?" And sometimes they say "Your project is not within our giving, are you sure you want to come?" But I continue listening. For example, with one foundation she started out by saying, "It's not really what we do," and then I teased her out and I said "What do you do, what are you working on?" And after a while, the conversation came around 180 degrees and she said, "Well, I would like to spend some time learning a bit more about your program."

Ask for Advice

We all know that if you want money, ask for advice. Occasionally, that's also effective with foundations as Marianne Lockwood mentioned.

Sometimes you can get a meeting with a program officer where you simply are asking to brainstorm or get advice where they wouldn't necessarily see you if it was clear that you were simply coming to them to make a request for money.

I have known some program officers who have been good about things and say, "Well, let's talk about who we know that could help you."

Cultivation Events

If your organization has interesting donor events consider putting program officers on your invitation list. Be careful, because some foundations specifically ask not to be invited to events.

However, Marianne Lockwood has numerous cultivation events for the orchestra, and she invites top prospects. But, "It's a long shot because if you do get somebody who agrees to come they know very well that they have been hooked. But sometimes it works."

Letters of Interest

One-page letters of interest describing a program, followed up by a phone call, are sometimes effective too.

What undergirds all of these approaches is integrity. Most people in a position to give money are clenched up inside knowing the world is trying to get something from them with smiles and flattery. Therefore, the most effective approach is to be straight-forward in your approach and honestly answer questions even if it's unflattering to your position.

Most people are surprised by honesty and really appreciate it.

What if the Fish Aren't Biting

Some foundations just don't respond however hard you try. I asked one of our master relaters, Mariann Payne, how she handles this.

> I move on. I just send it in writing if somebody really is just not going to sit down or take a call, I just follow their protocol and do it in writing and I move on to the next foundation on my list.
>
> I figure it's a crap shoot either way. Either they are going to read and be engaged by our proposal, or we're not going to get into the next phase of working with that foundation. And so many others need attention that I jump right on to the next one. I will try it but I won't put a lot of energy into it.

Initiating a conversation with a foundation is rarely easy as Marianne Lockwood points out, "It's hard and it takes a lot of work, so you really have to know that it's a good possibility and that it's a good fit because you are going to invest a lot of time and energy in cultivating them."

Luckily, many of us have enjoyed winning grants that started with a cold call or cultivation event. Once that happens a few times it gives you faith in the process and drives you to continue.

Questions to Consider

1. Are there any of the approaches listed above that I don't use? If so, could I put them in my arsenal and use them?

2. How persistent am I in creating relationships with funders? Do I put a lot of effort into getting acquainted before submitting something in writing or am I quick to jump to the writing stage?

3. Do we have a donor cultivation strategy for foundation officers and trustees that is as strong as for other major donors? If not, what could we put in place to strengthen it?

A Story: Grant Development as Connection

Once upon a time, not too long ago, a caterpillar was born. She lived a nice life eating her fill of luscious green leaves. After a couple of months, she started feeling sluggish so she found a beautiful tree and started spinning silk around her bulging frame. Slowly but surely, day after day, she spun and with each passing day she got more and more tired.

Finally, her cocoon was spun and she rested. Soft light filtered through the cocoon, and she drifted in and out of consciousness and finally went into a deep dream. The caterpillar's body liquefied until the cocoon was filled with a gel of undifferentiated cells.

Soon, a few cells differentiated themselves. These cells are called imaginals. They slowly connected and formed a web. Other cells joined the imaginals and little clusters began to take shape. Over the next few days, the clusters grew until the remaining cells could see their place in the new structure. When the cocoon saw the beautiful new creature it melted with joy and the most glorious butterfly flew out into the world.

I like to think that visionary nonprofit leaders and their counterparts at funding agencies are like imaginal cells. They see the possibility of a powerful new structure for our world and firmly hold that vision for others to coalesce around while waiting for the rest of humanity to catch up. Grant developers help create the connections between imaginals and open up the channels of communication so that they can clearly see each other.

Element 5

The "Getting to Know You" Process

Illustrates GPCI Competency

8.4. Identify methods of relationship cultivation, communication, recognition, and stewardship that might appeal to specific funders.

Getting a grant from a foundation ... is like dating by committee. If I wanted to ask you out ... I'd need to make a presentation to your first cousin, your first cousin is then going to talk to your mother, your dad, your brothers and sisters, and they are going to present my credentials and if I am approved you and I are going to get to go to the movies and dinner.... So that's why if someone doesn't know an organization or the request is large, or there is a lot of money involved, they may not want to take that first step yet.

John Hicks

Grant development is akin to dating. You spot a foundation or program that sparks your interest, and you invest time in learning about the foundation to see if you have anything in common.

Then you pluck up the courage to introduce yourself — and this may take several attempts as you engineer introductions from friends etc. Then you meet for a few dates and size each other up.

If things turn out well, you might commit to each other in the form of a small grant to see how it goes. If that works out well, you'll talk about the larger commitment of a big or multi-year grant.

So, how do top grant developers go about the early stages of courting foundations?

Do They Like Haiku or Tolstoy?

The first step in the process of getting to know someone is learning their likes and dislikes. Again, John Hicks has a wonderful analogy to describe this.

> Some people like Haiku and some people like prose. You have program officers who want everything in bullet points.

> I interviewed a program officer at the Kellogg Foundation...and he asked for 45 minutes. I get on the phone and he says "John, I have *16* minutes'" So, what have I learned in two seconds? He is a Haiku person. But if you really start thinking about the signals he is sending, that is an old counter interview trick.

> If I said to you "Jane, I have 16 minutes," you would pick the five most important things you wanted to learn from me. So, he's not only a person who likes Haiku, he's a person who values getting information in priority order.

> He's someone who is probably going to be looking at the fine print. These are the intangibles on how to write to him versus the guidelines for the Kellogg Foundation.

Sometimes, it's learning how to communicate with someone else that's the trick of the trade.

> "You have to let them decide the level of engagement and the kind of relationship they want to have. "
>
> Nancy Withbroe
> Share Our Strength

Do They Want to Invest or Partner?

In addition to honoring the program officer's personal preference for Haiku or Tolstoy, try to determine how the foundation perceives the grant, as Caitlin Stanton explains.

> Some foundations see this as a donation/investment. You need to articulate why that is a good donation, and you tell them the stories of impact that have come about because of that donation.
>
> With an institutional donor you are actually negotiating a partnership. It's important to understand the subtle differences between those two.

Investor/donor types give a grant to be part of your theory of change without further involvement other than a status report.

However, most corporations and some foundations consider that they are partners and have their own learning goals and expectations about return on investment in the form of clear deliverables. They often want more frequent updates and specific information, but that might not be clear unless you ask them. Nancy Withbroe also talked about this distinction and added,

Many of them really do want to be treated as partners in the process and want to be invited to substantive meetings where they can give input.

I just had a conversation with a funder last week where they have given us a major grant for a partnership...and we offered them the opportunity to come to a meeting sometime just to see the conversation, see how people are interacting and participate.

They were absolutely thrilled and didn't just want to be seen as writing a check and getting a couple of reports in writing and maybe a thank you meeting at the end where we are really asking them for money for the next time. They really appreciated the opportunity to be engaged.

Questions to Consider

1. Which of our potential funders want a partnership and which want to invest?
2. What opportunities can I create for relating differently with our partners and investors?
3. In what ways could I develop my listening and relational skills more fully? Some areas that you might want to look into are:
    - Neuro-linguistic programming
    - Active Listening
    - The Platinum Rule: Discover the Four Basic Business Personalities by Tony Alessandra and Michael J. O'Connor.

---○---

A Story: The Importance of Preference

I coordinated a very detailed proposal in the late 1990s for a multi-million dollar operating grant. The program officer at the time thought it was the best proposal he had ever read. It used a logic-model approach with goals/objectives/activities/evaluation metrics.

When that grant was about to expire, we used the same format to write another proposal to the same funder—but we worked with a different program officer. That reviewer thought the proposal was the worst he'd ever read—too detailed, not visionary enough. A few years and a new reader made a 180-degree turn in the subjective review from the program officer.

Melissa Brown,
Past Editor, *Giving USA*

---○---

Element 6

Finding and Empowering Your Champion in the Board Room

Imagine a board of trustees meeting: a dozen people sitting around a mahogany table coming together to talk about proposals that they've read or scanned over the last few weeks.

There's anticipation in the air and also hesitancy because they know that they simply can't fund everything. To win, you need to have someone sitting around that table that can advocate for your project, and top grant developers know it, as Mariann Payne explained.

> Find out what questions they are working on. See how you can interact so you can build a connection with the person who is going to be shepherding the proposal through and presenting it to the board.

> That has been really the most important time spent without a doubt over the past 20 years — the front work in building connections with the people behind the scenes at the foundations.

While program officers can be your champion and a powerful advocate for your organization within the boardroom, you really need to help them effectively do that. But how?

Bolster Their Agenda

Caitlin Stanton's organization, Global Fund for Women, makes small grants to women's groups worldwide, and she told me that she learned a lot from watching how her colleagues made funding decisions.

> I didn't understand when I first got started how sometimes program officers have an agenda within their foundations that can be a slightly shifted version of the stated public mission statement of the foundation.
>
> We do a lot of human rights work and sometimes the program officers that we work with are the people within those institutions who are trying to push a more progressive human rights focus agenda.
>
> So, how can we help them with their internal campaigns?

It's a great question. When you switch your mindset from "How can they help me?" to "How can I help them do their job?" there is a subtle shift in attitude and actions that creates a context of empowerment for everyone. Of course, first of all it requires getting to know the program officer well enough to ask what inspires them. John White shared his approach to engaging champions.

> I try to pass on the passion—you'll succeed if funders share your vision and mission and you get a champion within the organization. They won't be your champions unless they're lit up.
>
> So, think about what argument will excite people. I don't consciously look for one but once you have discovered who the program officer or the point person is, then I think it's quite important to try to

ensure that that person is as well informed as they can be about your organization and about the subject that you're dealing with.

As you begin to work on the proposal draft, ask your contact person what would be the most helpful to them in the board room. One of Caitlin's funders said, "Give me a couple of PowerPoint slides with some photos that I can present to the board. I can do the presentation and the talking."

Information Provider

Caitlin explained another role that non-profit staff members can play for program officers.

> They also really rely on grantees to be sources of information for them. So that has helped me think about our relationships with our donors.
>
> How can we not just submit the proposal but be a go-to source for a grassroots perspective on a specific issue when it comes up or help the folks within that foundation do their job better by getting them access to the kinds of information that they really want to have? And sometimes I hear our program officers are frustrated because they feel like they funded an organization and they are not getting this extra layer of information helping them be informed with the issues in general. I think that most nonprofits underestimate how their funding partners often crave learning more about what is happening in the field so that they can make smarter, more responsible decisions.

```
┌─────────────────────────────────────────────┐
│                                               │
│              10 QUESTIONS TO ASK              │
│              A PROGRAM OFFICER                │
│                                               │
│  1.  What perspective do you want?            │
│  2.  What's most compelling to you?           │
│  3.  Who else can I talk with, what else is   │
│      there to know?                           │
│  4.  What are you hoping to learn from this   │
│      grant?                                   │
│  5.  How can we be more accountable to you?   │
│  6.  What can I do to help you do your work   │
│      effectively?                             │
│  7.  What would success look like to you?     │
│      What would be most helpful to you?       │
│  8.  Is hearing about what we have been       │
│      learning important?                      │
│  9.  Would you like to hear about which of    │
│      our strategies do work and which don't,  │
│      or new innovations?                      │
│  10. Is learning more about the challenges    │
│      and progress in the field of interest    │
│      to you?                                  │
│                                               │
│              Shared by Caitlin Stanton,       │
│              Global Fund for Women.           │
│                                               │
└─────────────────────────────────────────────┘
```

Questions to Consider

1. Do I know what is important to program officers at current and potential funders?
2. In what ways could I boost their agendas?
3. What information do we have access to that funders might be interested in?
4. Have I asked them what format they would like information in?

5. What steps can I start taking now so that our organization has a champion in boardrooms that matter to us?

Grant Development as Sacred Service

We all fundamentally want the same thing: to live peacefully with people we love in a just world free from suffering. Values such as truth, love, compassion, courage, freedom, and justice are universal. I see grant development as a sacred service that opens up channels of communication for people's highest expression. At its core, the interaction between foundations and nonprofits is driven by our mutual desire to benefit the collective good.

For example, Foundation Y is deeply concerned about water. They have money but don't have the time, contacts, or expertise to implement programs. Non-Profit X is also concerned about our earth's waters. They have a huge network, passion, expertise and commitment but not the money.

In isolation, neither will be effective. But both groups desire the same thing and when money passes from one to another, it completes the circle and their intention is made manifest. When you look at it that way, program officers become peers with different resources than yours at their disposal and conversations have depth, authenticity, and urgency.

The state of the world poses some harsh realities. Working in grant development gives us the opportunity to be lovingly engaged in living a life aligned with higher values and assist others in doing the same. The freedom to do that is a privilege, and it is a gift to see it bear fruit.

Element 7

Four Ways to Respect Your Funders

Illustrates GPCI Competency

8.1. Identify characteristics of mutually beneficial relationships between fund seekers and funders.

Imagine that you could do a CAT scan and see each individual thought as it whizzes through top grant developer's brains. I'm pretty sure you'd see "What's important to you?" and "How can I help you?" more often than anything else.

They are exquisitely sensitive to funders and have a deep respect for them that is beyond the norm.

Respect their Intent

John White spent years in the British Diplomatic Corps before moving into development. As you'd expect, he's charm on two legs but underneath is a deep vein of respect.

> In the end you are dealing with people and very often people who have been very successful, very driven, and made a lot of money. They intend to do some good with this money, whatever good means, and they are going to jolly well make sure they do.

> I cannot help but respect somebody who has been hugely successful in their own professional life and then has the vision to find a way to improve the lives

of the rest of us and share the benefits of that success. There are some extraordinary people out there. But it is their money and you do have to respect that.

John and his ilk choose to focus on people's positive intentions rather than the mistakes they might make in execution of that intent. It is an attitude filled with acceptance for people's greatness and fallibility.

And it's so nice to be treated that way. It's no surprise to me that John raised over $40 million in four years for his organization. He probably conveys that genuine sense of respect in every one of his communications.

Respect their Power

I often hear grant developers complain about how XYZ foundation is capricious and the system is unfair.

Top grant developers don't say those things. For example, when I asked Jonathan Bank what irritated him about foundations he shot back "I try not to get aggravated by people who are giving me money."

Over and over again, I heard this same combination of

> "People who are successful in this grant writing business are not only able to be persuasive and to write clearly and to produce proposals that are going to work, but they are people who go beyond that and understand the human dynamics of the relationship once you are asking someone to back your particular proposal."
>
> John White
> Marine Stewardship Council

respect and total acceptance that they get to make the rules, as Bill Smith explained.

> You have no right to their money. They can be arbitrary. Never assume they are addicted to your cause, that you are the fairest of them all. Remember to ask if there's anything that you can do for them.

In the top grant developers' world there's no whining about capriciousness or stories about funders' arrogance.

We all have examples of less than desirable behavior but we choose to focus on funders' honorable intentions and the good that can be done by playing nicely in the sandbox.

If this underlying respect is absent in the grant development process, no amount of schmoozing or eloquent writing will get your proposal funded.

Respect them as People

Sue Caruso-Green was a Corporate Grants Officer with Citibank before moving into consulting and she lit up when I asked her what she learned from the ex- perience:

> "It is their money, they call the shots. Get over it."
> Sue Caruso-Green
> Non-Profit Central

> Funders are people too!!! Treat them with respect, not disdain.

> Remember to thank them when you get the grant, because they advocated for you and your cause.

> I can tell you the number of times people got back to me and said "Thank you so much, you were really so helpful to us." I don't mean the thank you "On behalf

of the such and such, thank you for your grant." A personal thanks.

So, why do we somehow lose our manners and capacity for compassion when we are interacting with people who hold the purse strings?

I think that there are a couple of things at play. First, many people think that there's a power disparity between the funder and the non-profit agency in a similar vein as the power disparity in a school. I think that this brings up our issues around power and authority and can lead to dehumanizing the authority figure, just as high schoolers dehumanize their teachers.

Second, money is our society's biggest taboo. Think about it, you probably know more about your friends' sex lives than you do about their financial picture. And most of us are uncomfortable with large sums of money and with asking for money.

I think that many people relate to program officers as their money rather than as people. When that happens, we forget normal civilities that we offer friends and colleagues.

But top grant developers never lose grasp of the fact that program officers and trustees are people first and donors second.

Respect Your Time and their Time

Mark Eiduson spent years as a foundation program officer and his tone was almost identical to Sue's when I asked him about the experience—bemusement at how uncivil people can be toward others who are trying to improve our world.

> People don't respect your time and many people don't know how to speak concisely. You don't have to do a three-minute elevator speech, but you need

to be able to speak briefly and compellingly or engagingly about your project. It is an art. It's not easy to speak very briefly and compellingly – it is a hard thing to do.

Sometimes it's tough to know when to accept "no" and when to probe a little more to see if there are potential connections between you and a funder.

But we can always bear in mind that for the person on the other end of the phone this is their 10th such call of the day, they have a site visit at 3 pm, and 15 proposals to review before tomorrow morning.

> "If people say they would like a regular call then give them one, act on it. But above all listen and the way to contend with a relationship is doing what people ask. It's no good putting in the thirty page report if they say to you 'that's very interesting and a lot of detail but actually all we want is the headline stuff...Listen and learn, I think is the way I would sum it up."
>
> John White
> Marine Stewardship Council

Questions to Consider

1. Can I speak compellingly and succinctly about our organization? If not, who could help me develop that skill? Consider joining Toastmasters to learn the art of persuasive speaking.
2. Do I routinely thank foundations for considering our proposals even when they are turned down?
3. Can I hear "no" when I pitch an idea and move on?

A Story of Perseverance

Twenty-five years ago we overreached artistically and financially. The organization risked folding and my whole board resigned.

I went to the foundation community who had been supporting us, and I managed to persuade them that they should give me an emergency grant and loan and become an advisory committee. And they did that.

I was also very lucky in that Harvey Lichtenstein had become a friend and chaired that committee. He was a true guardian angel. I don't think I would have had the nerve otherwise. His credibility made other people feel comfortable, that it was worth taking the risk to bail us out.

For six months, they served as a temporary board, helped me get out of debt, rebuild the board and ultimately turned the organization around, and we never looked back. To this day those foundations have remained major supporters and great friends. I still look back and wonder. I was pretty naïve and had no background in arts management. I was doing it all by the seat of my pants so I didn't know any better and as far as I was concerned, I had nothing to lose. That they took the risk was pretty astonishing. For me, it comes down to really believing in your mission and also having a great deal of patience and persistence.

We should have given up and gone bankrupt but we didn't. We don't fit any model because I didn't know that we were supposed to fit any model.

Marianne Lockwood
Founder, Orchestra of St. Luke's, New York

Element 8

Why You Should Always Contact Government Program Officers

Illustrates GPCI Competency

1.04. Identify techniques to learn about specific funders.

Government bureaucrats are paid with our tax dollars. Unlike foundation program officers they are public servants and their job is to serve Congress and U.S. tax-payers — you and me.

> "Ask Government Program Officers "Who else should I talk to?"
>
> Ann Redelfs

If you are preparing a government proposal make sure that you take advantage of this by talking with the program officer responsible. It's well worth your time.

Ann Redelfs is a 6-foot tall blonde powerhouse who lives along the icy shores of Minnesota's Lake Superior. She has spent her professional career in a male-dominated field–the hard sciences. She works on large multi-institutional scientific proposals to the National Science Foundation (NSF) and other government agencies that are considered the toughest nuts to crack. I suspect that little intimidates Ann and her no-nonsense approach to these calls.

I am not afraid at all to make call to program officers...I will call them and say "I am talking to this group of individuals about a proposal for your RFP XYZ and I have some questions for you."

I send an email first and ask, "When may I call you?" It's my expectation that they're there to help us, and I that's always proven to be true—they're dedicated and ready to offer honest opinions and good advice.

I am still astounded at how some people feel they shouldn't call the program officer of the grant. They feel like it is getting inside information and that is exactly the wrong way to look at that.

The right way to look at this is the more information you can get from the program officer, the more you are going to realize whether or not it's worth your time to work on that proposal.

She also has a habit that I added to my repertoire with great results.

Always ask, "Who else should I talk to?" Because someone will always lead you to someone else who will give you more advice. I can't tell you how priceless it is to do that.

I know people who will write an entire proposal and submit it and have never spoken to the program officer at all and I think, "You could have made your proposal so much stronger by asking questions of the people who know what's going on." It amazes me.

Questions to Consider

1. Do I routinely call government program officers during the proposal development stage? If not, what is holding me back? What is that costing me?

2. How could our grant development be improved if we made it a matter of routine to speak to program officers?

PROGRAM AND PROJECT DESIGN

To the average person, planning isn't the sexiest thing on the planet. But talk to a top government grant developer and you'll get a whole different perspective.

Just as foundation grant developers are relationship gurus, government grant developers get a high from executing a complex project with precision and grace.

In this section, we'll talk about the tricks that they use to keep projects fun, thrilling, and on track...most of the time.

> "I thought of writing as a solitary endeavor. Proposal writing is coordinating a process that involves a team of people, and then writing the results in a unified voice for the funder's guidelines. I hadn't expected to be coordinating a team."
>
> Melissa Brown
> Past Editor, *Giving USA*

---○---

What is a Grant Proposal?

Dear Santa,

We have been good. We need defibrillators, please. This is a request for $50,000. Please send it to us.

Sincerely,
Non-profit

Proposals are not letters to Santa. A grant proposal is basically a plan for creating change in which you are trying to convince a funder to invest.

It must reflect strong planning supported by data. A strong competitive grant proposal reflects good planning, contains easy-to-understand data, and tells a story.

The biggest misunderstanding about grant development is that its success is dependent on the writing.

If I had a dollar for every time that someone has asked me to "Just write a proposal" as if "write" were the operative word, I'd be able to keep myself in designer clothing for the rest of my life.

Frank Mandley
Frank Mandley & Associates

---○---

Element 9

Getting Your Team Thinking

Illustrates GPCI Competencies

3.01. Identify methods of soliciting and incorporating meaningful substantive input and contributions by stakeholders, including client groups, beginning with the development of a new concept or program.

2.05. Identify values, purposes, and goals of fund-seeking entities' overall strategic plans in the grants process

Walk into a room of nonprofit staff and tell them that you've got a good shot at a $500,000 grant, and their ears will perk up. After their heart skips a few beats some will start spouting their department's shopping list.

But since proposals are not letters to Santa, our job is to lead the conversation away from "What stuff shall we buy?" to "What can we achieve? What's the best way of accomplishing that?"

But how do you get busy people to think a project through from A-Z quickly, clearly and creatively?

Here are top grant developers' favorite strategies.

Getting Your Team Thinking Strategy 1: Reignite their passion and keep them focused on the problem

I find that people working in the social sector are misty-eyed idealists at heart but years of working in underfunded systems saps their energy and disconnects them from their dreams.

When people are used to living in an environment of insufficiency they often think that buying stuff will fix the problem.

Top grant developers have a knack for reconnecting people with their inner-idealist and then pumping them to fill in the details of how they will realize their dreams.

I work to get teams to forget about what normally constrains them—time and money—in order to relax into brainstorming.

I tell my clients to imagine that I have just won the lottery, and that I love and believe in them so much that I'm going to give them the check. They can use it how they want and it will be approved by all the powers that govern their field. It often takes a little guidance and prodding to keep them veering off into "We can't do that because..." thinking but it usually leads to some great ideas.

But before you can come up with inspiring solutions you also need

"We make people think. A lot of times there has been an idea that has been floating around in their head in a vague way for years maybe and we make them sit down, get with other people from other departments, and really try to formulate what it is they really want to do."

Mary Knepper
St. Joseph's Hospital
Health Center

to articulate the root causes of the problem. Johna Rodgers has worked for years for a school consortium in Kentucky and knows this problem well.

> I constantly have got to make them think about what is possible, not what they don't have, but how to focus on what they need and how to remedy that.

> They are so used to "No, no, no" that they can't see past the "Well you know if we had a computer lab." No. I promise you Caesar didn't have a computer lab, and he was a pretty smart guy. There have been geniuses that didn't have computers, how did they get there? There has got to be a way to do it.

> I keep them focused on the need, the need, the need, by constantly asking, "What is the problem?"

Sue Caruso-Green uses a similar approach by, saying in her Brooklyn twang, "So who cares? What's the big deal if we don't get this money? What is going to go wrong with the world if we don't get the money? Assuming we are not going to get the money, what would be the big deal? Life will go on, right?" Doing this helps her clients get down to the real reason why the funder should make the grant.

Getting Your Team Thinking Strategy 2: Linking need, approach, outcome chart

Most people seem to know what they want to do and what they want to buy, but they are often much less clear about why they want to do so, or what results they will get by doing so. They tend to "intuit "the problem and "opine" the solution rather than support the problem or need to be addressed with data and provide a justification, based in research or practice, that the methods or activities to be implemented are a good choice and have a reasonable chance of resolving the problem.

Frank Mandley

Sue Caruso-Green shared a deceptively simple model to overcome this issue and help people relate the problem to proposed methods and outcomes. She uses a table akin to a logic model that she calls the NAO approach that looks like this:

Need	Activity	Outcome/Year

Sue's simple NAO chart helps groups to think through the grant activities and also provides a point of discipline since she insists that no activity can be included without linking it to a need or outcome. It looks really basic but just the act of fully completing it will bring a project out of the ether and into concrete terms in a short order.

Getting Your Team Thinking Strategy 3: Follow the Money

Fifteen years ago, I was told by a program officer to "follow the money" and that comes back to me constantly...and when I am preparing to write the grant I really put down the dollars we need for each thing and I walk through the program from day one. So I can show how the money will be spent and how it will impact the project. I always explain exactly what the funds will be used for and to make it very clear...it makes a big difference.

Alice Boyd

I'm sure that Alice uses this insight as a planning tool with her clients by asking them, what will you do on day 1, in month 1, first quarter etc. and then attach expenses to each of the activities. Combining the NAO approach with "following the money" is a powerful combination.

> "People have the kernel of an idea and they have figured out that they want to get from to A to Z. I help them to think about B through Y."
>
> Diane Gedeon-Martin
> The Write-Source

Getting Your Team Thinking Strategy 4: Elementary Strategic Planning

While large proposals absolutely require complex planning and active management, it's possible to let that slide when working on smaller foundation proposals for tiny nonprofits. But, that would be a mistake as Nancy Withbroe pointed out.

I think the most important thing for the organization to do first is to have a clear strategic plan even if it's just three pages and they don't have the time to go through some multi-year complicated process with a consultant.

Even if it's just sitting in a room with a board and staff leaders are articulating these are our priorities, these are our visions, what we want to do in the next three years, or five years and have that drive the fundraising. If you don't have that then you are just going to be all over the place.

The idea of simple strategic planning for small non-profits that doesn't take days and weeks to accomplish perked my interest, and so I delved a little deeper and she explained how she leads her organization through the process.

Nancy starts off by explaining that most nonprofits are touching on other issues and connecting with others beyond their core focus. Then she helps the team open up to who they are and what they do from lots of different perspectives.

She told me that she uses four core questions to get them thinking in this direction.

1. Who are our audiences?
2. Who are our secondary audiences?
3. Whose lives are touched by the work that we do?
4. What are the issue areas that you touch — be inclusive here, for example a meal program with a service learning project with middle schoolers could ask for funding from organizations that aren't interested in food or the population served but interested in kids and social awareness. In this example, the organization does food delivery, advocacy and education.
5. Then she follows up with,
6. Based on answers to these four questions, what is our vision five years from now?
7. Given that, what are our fundraising priorities?

Nancy's approach helps tiny organizations clarify who they are, what they do, why, and where they are headed. This clear thinking will shine through in any written document.

While it's tempting to jump into the writing as soon as possible, top grant developers know that time invested in planning will pay off in the long-term with more funded proposals and better run programs.

Questions to Consider

1. What helps my team get in the brainstorming flow?
2. How can I make the brainstorming process more fun?
3. Do I always ensure that my team fills in missing details in the planning or do I prefer to let some details slide because I'm not willing to be seen as antagonistic?
4. Do we have an organizational strategic plan to help guide grant development? If not, who do I need to talk with to put that ball in motion?

A Story: Keeping the Dream Alive

The most rewarding job of my career was working with a hospital administrator who had dreamed of co-locating children's primary and mental health care for 25 years.

I worked on a proposal with her that would allow that to happen for the first time in New York State. There are all kinds of regulatory barriers that make it no simple task. She had submitted proposals before that were turned down and couldn't get internal funding.

Our proposal was funded. I get a huge amount of satisfaction knowing that our work together will result in a new model of caring for children in the state that will reduce the stigma of seeking mental health care.

My ability to revive the notion that it really was possible and to help her muster the energy for yet another try paid off.

I encourage you to find your own way of getting people to put down their "can'ts" for a while and focus on what could be done and why it's worth doing.

Element 10

Promise Only What You Can Deliver

It's always tricky to know exactly how much to promise in a proposal. You don't want to sound as though it's going to be a bad return on investment, but you also don't want to bite off more than you can chew and under-deliver.

So how do you find that delicate balance? By planning carefully and erring on the side of caution. Frank Mandley worked in a large school district for decades and has plenty of examples of when poor planning took its toll.

> Often naïve grant developers either promise the moon and the stars to funders and can't deliver or they completely underestimate the amount of work they are taking on.

> A grant developer in our district committed to implementing a new intervention model with a control group of 1,000 comparable students to determine its effect...it was difficult to find 100 control group students, much less a thousand!

The cost of such a mistake is hours of time spent on phone calls, amendments, and the possibility of creating a bad reputation with funders.

While some people might be tempted to make big promises, funders have a very good sense of what is feasible and view grandiose promises as a sign of lack of expertise.

Marilyn Zlotnik, Vice President of Metis Associates, is a smart ambitious New Yorker who can run rings around most arguments. She is also the child of two public school teachers and is deeply committed to ensuring that high-quality public education exists for our children.

She works exclusively with school districts and is all too familiar with some people's desires to over-promise. She said, "Don't feel that you have to promise to change the world to get the grant. Being realistic and being specific is really what convinces reviewers. Don't be overly ambitious."

Questions to Consider

1. In what circumstances is my team tempted to over-promise?
2. During the program planning process, if we develop a new program and don't know what a realistic deliverable is, which peers can we ask for their advice?

A Story: The Enabler

The biggest mistake of my career was to offer too much planning help to an organization that didn't have the experience, drive, or knowledge to plan the program on their own.

I was hired by a senior executive and worked almost exclusively with her and a few select members of her team.

The rationale was that they had applied for funding before and it became a planning nightmare with lots of competing agendas. Limiting the process seemed expedient. I gave them lots of advice about program design.

They won a multi-million dollar grant but by the time it was funded all but one of the people who I had worked with had left the organization. No one who was charged with implementing the grant had any clue about its content or commitment to its success.

They totally failed to execute the program and the grant was rescinded. By trying to help too much, I inadvertently damaged the agency's reputation, caused them to waste time that could have been used serving their clients, and shattered their faith in their own ability to succeed in the grants game.

It was a hard lesson to learn but now I make sure that I empower my clients but never enable them to do something that they wouldn't be able to conceive of and implement in my absence.

Element 11

The Art of Eliciting Information from Very, Very, Very Busy People

Illustrates GPCI Competency

3.01. Identify methods of soliciting and incorporating meaningful substantive input and contributions by stakeholders, including client groups, beginning with the development of a new concept or program.

Most nonprofit staff members do a great impression of the Roadrunner these days, running from one meeting or crisis to the next.

One of the biggest hurdles that grant developers face is getting information from busy people. Many come to meetings and brainstorm but when it comes down to ferreting out some data buried on the their hard drive or making a phone call to a colleague across town for comparative data they put it on the back burner.

Top grant developers shared three approaches that they use to get information back on their desks: a) flexing to other people's preferred style; b) explaining why you need their help; and c) providing a fill-in-the-blanks template.

Appealing to Their Style

Most people are extremely over-worked. Recognizing this, top grant developers have learned to make it as easy as possible for people to contribute. As Diane Gedeon-Martin said, "We must adapt to their style, not the other way around, when we are leading a team."

Mary Knepper works in a large hospital and comes across this problem a lot. She seems to intuitively find the path of least resistance, "Some people prefer phone, others email and some in-person meetings. Figure out what they prefer and then give it to them that way. Some people want to be interviewed."

People skills are just as important as planning skills when it comes to getting big grant proposals done.

Educating the Team about the Process

John Hicks emphasized how putting a lot of time into setting up the scene for his team both saved time and produced results.

> The more people understand what the funder is requesting and why the funder is requesting, it will help them understand what you are doing and why you are doing it.

> I spend a lot of time talking to program staff. I say, "I have some things I need to do with you and I am probably going to need an hour of your time. I know you are incredibly busy. Let me tell you about the grant maker, let me tell you about what they are looking for, and I think an hour will be worth it because then I will not have to come back and bother you."

> The more they are attuned to why we are doing what we are doing the better it goes.

Fill In the Blanks Templates

Appealing to someone's higher nature doesn't work when they are already running flat out saving the world as Mary Knepper knows, "Nobody here has time to read the whole RFP. A lot of times I will give it to them but if I try to take things from the RFP and say, 'You do this and you do that or I need your help with this,' it doesn't really work." And she is right; sometimes it just doesn't work to cajole people for information.

She told me about a technique that does work.

> What I have found works the best is if I set up a template of the proposal.
>
> I type the question and I leave a half page blank, so that they can see there is information that has to go in that spot and they can see the question we have to respond to.
>
> Then we go through and put the names into that template and they can take it back and say, "Okay, here is what I need to work on, number 1 and number 5 and number 10."
>
> And then they can fill in the blanks and when that document begins to grow they can feel that accomplishment and they can see where the holes are.

Mary isn't talking about asking her team to write entire sections but it gives her some draft language that she can work from to develop a cohesive whole. It's a deceptively simple idea based on the understanding that we naturally like things to be whole and complete and so leaving a blank spot calls out to us at a gut level.

Sometimes the simplest approaches are the most effective.

Questions to Consider

1. When my team is running flat out do I explain why I need the information?
2. Do I know how different members of my team prefer to share information? Consider taking an hour to ask each person in your team what they prefer.
3. Would the template approach work with my team?

Element 12

Government Grant Developers' Dominatrix Gene

Illustrates GPCI Competency

4.3. Identify work strategies for submitting high-quality proposals on time.

Preparing a large government proposal in a matter of a few weeks requires almost military-grade planning. For survival, all government grant developers are sticklers for creating detailed timelines.

But sticking to a timeline and still having a functional team is an art. Successful grant developers use two parts charm, one part persistence, and one part threat to get the job done.

Alice Boyd is a creative, smart, and highly successful consultant based on Cape Cod who hit the nail on the head when talking about keeping projects on track.

> I am a kind and courteous taskmaster, like a dominatrix.
>
> You have to be kind and courteous and appeal to everyone, but you have to hold that whip. I give them due dates, I provide reminders and when they forget, I call them and I give them a face-saving way to get it done.

There are times when you have to call their bluff. I am the first one to say "This is going to get into the press if we don't get this particular thing done and this is not going to reflect well on you and what can I do to make this better?"

So it is managing people but it is also holding the whip.

The dominatrix gene runs pretty strongly through the grant developer race. Alan Tiano and Marilyn Zlotnik both described how they kindly but firmly keep projects moving forward.

If I don't get a preliminary budget by the due date, I call that person directly and say, "You are responsible for this" and they say, "Oh, I gave that to somebody else," but I say, "No, you are responsible for it. This is what you agreed upon when we started. Where's the work?"

You have got to be tough sometimes. I will be bad cop as long as the stuff gets done on time. (Alan)

It's always a hard thing, setting boundaries with clients. Managing client expectations is the hardest thing about our business.

I tend to have a little bit less of a hard time with it because for whatever reason, they listen to me. I am the enforcer. The kids listen to me, the clients listen to me, I guess I have an authoritative tone to my voice or whatever, but not everybody can do that. (Marilyn)

But dominatrices have a heart and know when to push their clients and when to charm them. Top grant developers do the same. They routinely set false deadlines to give themselves wiggle room and they know when to use it.

When I asked Marilyn if she ever gives way, she told me, "I do bend when the client panics, is bordering on hysterical, or when you can see that they are very stressed there is no reason to have them be in that state." And Alan also showed that same depth of compassion.

> Bless their hearts, they are each working two FTEs, they are doing many more services with much less money, they are all overworked, they are burning out and you come in and you start demanding more work from them. And you have to keep that in mind. But at the same time if you want the funding, you have to get this stuff done.

The bottom line is getting the proposal done and submitted even it means ruffling a few feathers. Marilyn has raised more than $200 million dollars in her 25-year career and her work makes a big difference to the communities she works with. She told me,

> There is a self-preservation aspect to this though, too. With one client recently, I gave up my weekend and made myself available to him morning, noon and night. But when I told him that 4:30 pm was my deadline for input, I did not move off of my dime. I had something at my kid's school, and I hadn't been to my kid's school in three months.
>
> I drew the line in the sand. That is keeping that balance. Keeping that work-life balance is the thing that gives me the stamina to do five multi-million proposals in the space of two months.

By setting boundaries she preserves her ability to keep writing top-notch grant proposals long after most of her competition has burned out.

Questions to Consider

1. Do I always create a detailed timeline when planning government or large foundation proposals?
2. Am I willing to challenge people when they don't send something to me as promised? How can I do that clearly but kindly?
3. Am I letting too much slide with people and allowing the process to be more stressful than it needs to be?
4. If I'm not comfortable being an enforcer, is that something I am willing to develop or am I unsuited to that type of work environment?

"In talking about deadlines I bring it into weeks rather than months. For example, telling someone that it's due in 12 weeks sounds a lot closer than three months. It seems to get people moving faster. At the end of each email I put how many weeks 'til the deadline."

Ann Redelfs
Redelfs LLC

---◯---

Time as Self-Awareness

The foundation of time management is self-awareness. To manage your time effectively, you need to know what things you like, what you will avoid if allowed, what is your most productive time of day and how long things take you. Ann Redelfs summed this up beautifully. "Know your own schedule and the best time to work. Know your own rhythm and what you are willing to sacrifice."

One of my teachers spent years coaching small business owners and realized that people routinely underestimate how long things will take by a factor of three. If I think it will take an hour to write a section, it's more likely to take three.

He said that it was uncanny that this seemed to be universally true. It's not that some people underestimate by a factor of two or six; uniformly we all tend to underestimate by a factor of three. When I'm planning a task, unless I know for sure how long it will take, I take a guess and then multiply by three. Works like a dream.

---◯---

Element 13

Three Ways to Nurture Strong Collaborations

Illustrates GPCI Competencies

3.2. Identify methods of building partnerships and facilitating collaborations among applicants.

8.3. Identify methods to help fund-seeking organizations create effective collaborations with other organizations appropriate to funders' missions and goals.

The tighter money gets, the more funders favor multi-agency collaborations over single agency grant submissions. Funders always favor mergers and collaborations in economic downturns. If getting a grant is like dating, creating collaborative proposals is like getting married. You can expect disagreements about the dress, who sits at the top table, and whether the children will be raised Catholic or Jewish. So, what do the pros know about pulling it all off without a hitch and creating a marriage that endures long past the wedding?

> "The biggest problem when working with non-profits is turf battles - who gets to be in charge, who gets the money, who decides what the collaborative program is going to be."
>
> Dory Rand
> The Woodstock
> Institute

Expect Turf Battles

You would think that because of their intrinsic altruism people in non-profits would be temperamentally better suited to playing nicely in the sandbox. But human beings are wired to be territorial. At our basest level we are tribal beings with a two-year old's urge to grab a toy and say "mine."

One of my college professors was an expert in Eastern European relations and in the early 1990s was immersed in the boundary struggles in the former Yugoslavia. She told us that she would talk to people and read accounts of tribalism and shake her head in disbelief that educated people behaved this way.

Then her next-door neighbor put a fence around his yard and inadvertently fenced in one of her trees. She told us that right then, she got it. Her reaction was an immediate and powerful indignation followed by an urge to retaliate.

Of course, she controlled the urge and sorted it out peacefully, but I think it is a great example of the tribal programming that we all carry—even non-profit leaders.

Top grant developers seem to have a clear understanding and acceptance of this reality as Mark Eiduson acknowledged. "Collaboration takes time and trust and that is very, very difficult for nonprofits where there is a tendency toward competition and independence."

Once you accept that territorialism is alive and well in nonprofits, you can then move ahead within that context and find solutions and pathways to progress.

How to Bring People to the Table

The first step in building a collaboration can sometimes be the most difficult—bringing people to the table.

One way that top grant developers do this is by talking about the benefits of collaboration. Alice Boyd said that she "can get people who haven't had a civil conversation in years to come to the table by focusing on benefits. My goal is to make everyone feel and look good and improve the community's reputation."

Mark Eiduson takes a similar tack with his multi-agency collaboration.

> This organization has developed an approach to collaboration that has worked well over the past 10 years or so and that is that no money gets put on the table when the groups come together.
>
> So there is nothing in it for anybody except doing a better job and that's what brings them out...we take the approach that we don't have any money to put into this right now but there is work we can do better together that none of us is going to be able to accomplish alone. So, we agree to come together to work better and we will look for the funding along the way.

You can see that these two highly successful grant developers don't use the bait of money to get people to participate.

By calling on people's higher selves they engage people who are intrinsically motivated by societal change rather than those who are motivated by cash. When there's work to be done and compromises to be made, the folks who are in it to help others and build their organizations over the long term will flex whereas those who are there for this year's budget will just walk away.

What To Do When Your Partnership is Lopsided

Coalitions often form where the members vary in size, influence, and money. This can lead to lopsided relationships where one party feels powerless.

However, those of us who have worked for large institutions know how much leverage the little guys have.

I talked with Ann Redelfs about a friend who runs a non-profit that partners with a large university and originally felt as though it was a lopsided relationship in which the university wasn't contributing as much as it could to the partnership. She got truly animated and told me that non-profits needed to do six things.

Change Your Attitude

When you have the "Please sir, may I have some more?" attitude you fail to realize that your partner needs your help. One day 50 years ago when Habitat for Humanity started, it was ten people sitting around a church in Atlanta, Georgia. And they had a "Please sir may I have some more?" mindset, too, but they've changed that and are a powerful organization that others want to support—you, too, must shift your attitude to be a powerful peer.

Know the Power of What You Offer

Realize, and have the attitude, that what you are doing is absolutely critical and it will make a difference in people's lives and then go after those partners that will help you achieve that vision.

Don't let anyone make you feel that they are big and you are little. You are the 800-pound gorilla because you're the one with the vision, the dream, and the passion. You're the one who is committed to making this happen, and it won't materialize without your enthusiasm.

Be a Positive Force in the Universe

Large institutional partners are going to benefit from partnerships with small agencies that are doing valuable work, spade after spade, after spade.

Know that the larger organization will mention how they partner with your community-based organization in every foundation grant they write for the next decade. What is that kind of good press worth to them?

Do Something Physically that Makes You Feel Powerful and Strong

Take a very big deep breath and sit up as straight as you can and make the call.

Talk Plainly

Just say, "Not enough is happening here yet and I know you want this to happen, too. I think it's in your best interest to see this succeed. I know you believe in this, and we need to expand, we need to evolve and I need more resources. What are we going to do about that?" Then wait quietly for their response.

Move Up or Move On

If they are willing to step forward that's wonderful. If not, then you now know something. Knowledge is power. Move on.

By bringing people to the table, being aware of turf battles and striving to build long-term equitable relationships built on clear communication, top grant developers help to build powerful coalitions and shore up the chances of developing successful grant proposals.

Questions to Consider

1. Does my organization put the time and effort into building long-term partnerships that can be the basis for stronger grant submissions? If not, is that something that would strengthen our capacity to offer services?

2. How often do we come together for grant development without having a solid working partnership in place first?

3. What community collaborations does my organization participate in?

4. Are there unmet needs in our community that could be best served through a community-wide collaboration?

MAKING A CASE
AND WRITING
THE APPLICATION

Element 14

The Power of Story: Writing a Bodice-Ripping Romance

Illustrates GPCI Competency

4.6. Identify proposal writing approaches, styles, tones, and formats appropriate for proposing organizations and various audiences.

Alice Boyd runs a successful grant development business and takes her work seriously. She is a beautiful woman in her 50s and when you meet her you are struck by her poise, no-nonsense attitude, and a professionalism that draws on a deep well of experience.

She is known for her success in writing Housing and Urban Development proposals, which are notoriously long, involve detailed forms, and ask dry, tedious questions.

I was simply astonished when she told me how she thinks about her work.

> We approach each project as if we were writing a romance novel. In each grant you need action, you need a hero, and you need an undercurrent of passion. You need to woo the reviewer and keep him interested, and you want to flirt a bit.

> Then you need to make them confident that you'll deliver. I am a passionate person, and I won't take a project unless I can really get into it and feel the love. So we build our grants as if we are building romance novels.

After some time I managed to stop laughing long enough to begin appreciating the wisdom wrapped within the humor. Alice understands the power of storytelling, the importance of love, and the need for humor in our work.

In this chapter, we'll consider the power of storytelling and leave the love and humor for later.

> "I am trying to seduce the funder. I know that and so I want to give them that little bit of seduction. When you think about a new relationship, when you meet someone and there's that undercurrent of like 'woo' and that is what I want to provide. I want funders to really want us, really want to fund our project. I want them to think that this is going to be really good."
>
> Alice Boyd
> Bailey Boyd Associates

Finding the Story

Jean Houston said that if aliens came to earth and asked who we are, the most universal description is that we are storytellers.

We all tell stories about our lives, our families, and our communities. Our religions and cultures are passed from generation to generation through story.

Jonathan Bank is a masterful storyteller and grant developer. He is a theater director in New York City and when I first asked if I could interview him, he said he didn't have much to say. But his name had been given to me by a foundation program officer as one of her best grantees, and so I assumed that she saw something in his approach that he wasn't acknowledging to me. We agreed to talk with the understanding that if I didn't find the interview useful, I could toss it away.

It turns out that Jonathan has the most unusual approach to grant writing of all the interviewees.

He told me that years ago, he attended a workshop in which they explained that the skills he used as an artistic director were also relevant and useful in the fundraising arena. So he purposefully uses his artistic talents when he writes grant proposals.

> When I am ready to start rehearsing a play I begin by saying "This is the story of X." I often begin with that sentence or that fragment of a sentence.

> When I begin creating the text that will end up in a grant, I am not thinking about raising money. I am thinking, "What is the story of this play?"

> Whether I am working on a marketing piece or a fundraising piece, I understand that I am telling a story. I think about structure and what makes for good storytelling in the theatre.

> So with a grant it might be "How do I make sure the first act sets forth an engaging conflict that will make the audience want to come back and see the play after intermission or will make you want to continue reading the proposal — that it will make you go to the next section to continue reading?"

I found the interview with Jonathan invaluable not only because of his conscious use of storytelling but also how he demonstrates that while many people have the skills to write proposals they don't realize it.

For example, Linda Butler was a social worker before becoming a grant developer and pointed out that social workers are trained to listen to and engage clients but often fail to use that skill to build relationships with program officers. The skills that theater directors use for casting are equally useful in building a grant development team.

Top grant developers know that they must stir the readers' hearts and souls enough to for them to take action.

A foundation program officer once told me "I got down on my knees to beg for that one." As a federal reviewer I've also stuck my neck out to advocate for proposals by pointing out their strengths when I felt that my colleagues were grading them too harshly.

But it takes courage to do that. Telling a great story is the easiest and least threatening way to engage someone in your work so that they might consider advocating for you.

Stories are not about words but about images. What pictures do you paint in your grants?

Questions to Consider

1. Do I think about my grant proposals as telling a story?
2. Who could I toss story ideas around with when I am writing?
3. What is my organization's story? Try telling a story about your organization to a friend or colleague using the main story elements:
    *   Characters — hero, heroine, or villain
    *   Setting — paint a picture
    *   Plot — sequential and clear
    *   Conflict — problem that you address leading to a climax
    *   Resolution
4. When I write do I question, "Is this compelling enough for them to want to keep reading?" If the answer is no, be willing to be a brutal editor.

For more information, refer to Storytelling for Grantseekers by Cheryl Clarke.

---○---

The Art of Enough

The art of writing is leaving enough space and even a little mystery in the document. Good grant proposals make people think. Is it enough to get them interested?

It isn't going to answer every question because you don't know what the questions are. If three people read a proposal we would have three different sets of questions, and it's impossible to predict what questions a reviewer will have unless they talked to us before they finished; hence the reason talking to your reader before you submit can really be a good idea.

If you think about good relationships, think about the experience you have when you sit down with somebody and they talk at you versus someone who talks to you, who leaves silences, asks questions, draws you into a conversation versus the approach that "I am going to tell you everything."

Which is more appealing?

John Hicks
J.C. Geever, Inc.

---○---

Element 15

Mastering the Art of Persuasion

Illustrates GPCI Competencies

9.3 Organize ideas appropriately
9.4. Convey ideas clearly
9.5. Make a persuasive argument

If you took a time machine back to 1984 and went into the Nottingham High School for Girls auditorium on a Wednesday at lunchtime you would have found me in a decidedly unappealing blue school uniform enthusiastically debating the existence of God or the efficacy of non-violent resistance with a team from the boys' school across the road.

While my debating prowess and ghastly school uniform did very little to improve my ability to get a date, the former has stood me in good stead as a grant developer. I have a keen sense for engaging the audience, choosing just the right points to make at the right time, and zeroing in on the crux of the matter so that I can make a counterpoint in a flash.

When storytelling that evokes emotion is coupled with logical argument you have a compelling grant proposal.

More than half the people I interviewed had received formal or informal training in the art of persuasion. Many were in school debate teams or were raised in a family of lawyers. Alice Boyd said that

> Our evening dinner table growing up was a training ground for vigorous and impassioned debate. To this

day our family breaks every rule during dinner, hotly debating politics and religion throughout the meal and for hours afterwards.

In fact, my youngest brother who is an ardent Republican receives constant e-mails and phone solicitations from every liberal fundraising organization thanks to my generosity with his name.

Mariann Payne brought the importance of rhetoric to my attention when we talked about where the artistry lay in grant development.

There is a myth that there is a magic bullet that will win any grant. I think there isn't a magic formula. It is very hard to teach someone a) how to write, and b) how to write with conviction about the case that you are trying to gain support for.

In the early days of my doctoral studies, we studied the rhetoric of Aristotle and we did a lot of work on appealing to the ethos of the speaker or the audience. We have lost that rhetorical background and training.

Rhetoric is "the art of influencing the thought and conduct of an audience." That could also stand as a good definition of grant development.

Aristotle's rhetorical approach has three main elements: one must appeal to an audience's ethos (beliefs or ideals), logos (reason), and pathos (emotion).

Ethos is asking the audience to consider your credibility in assessing your argument. In grant dev-elopment, this means making a strong case for your team's expertise in program development and grant man-agement. When you successfully appeal to the reviewer's ethos, you have enough standing with them that you can give the essential details and they trust you to fill in the rest.

Pathos is engaging the reader on a heart-level and involves searching the depths of your own soul about you what you want to convey as well as trying to understand what will speak to the reviewer's deepest held beliefs and ideals. You can do this by thinking about what makes the reviewers tick, what their lives are like, and how they feel and might respond. This work is both intuitive and intellectual.

Logos is deductive reasoning. In grant development this is presenting a sound and logical plan that the reviewer can see is achievable.

When combined with an engaging story these elements create compelling arguments that win grant funding, if not a date in high school.

> "I am a subtle observer of human nature and narrative and am attenuated to language and its beauty and the power of it to change perspective. Through the use of artful precise language you can move an audience or get somebody to call you back, or win an argument...It's the art of persuasion. I have a fire in the belly to promote this in a way that will make it compelling. I think you need the ability to grow in knowledge and wisdom and to be able to write with maturity so that you are a good distiller of the truth."
>
> Mariann Payne
> Woodstock Theological Center

Question to Consider

1. Do I enjoy playing with arguments and finding the most persuasive way to present something? If not, consider joining Toastmasters. Their focus is on oral presentation,

but you'll get lots of practice in presenting a case for support.

If you would like to refresh your knowledge of rhetorical argument try *A Rulebook for Arguments* by Anthony Weston.

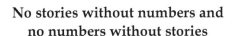

**No stories without numbers and
no numbers without stories**

My rule is no stories without numbers and no numbers without stories. It's very important to include those personal stories of change, to weave in the numbers as indicators but never to just throw them in there without a context and meaning of what is behind them.

And when we are crafting this narrative of the proposal or report, understand what is the donor's role in that narrative and weave them into that story too.

Caitlin Stanton
Global Fund for Women

Element 16

Be Crystal Clear

I do a lot of training and I edit stuff for my teachers out in the field. That makes me better because when their first sentence is, "The rolling hills of Lovely County Kentucky," I go "OK, let's stop right there. How did that just help your kids?" Yes, we need to paint a picture, but we need to paint a picture somewhere else. Don't let your first sentence be lame. Don't use it unless it's going to bring them in, unless it's going to be capturing and make them want to read it.

Johna Rodgers

When Sue Caruso-Green worked at Citibank she was on the receiving end of 'rolling hills of Kentucky' type proposals and can attest to their complete inefficacy.

I remember opening up packages and thinking, "What do these people want? How much do they want? What category do I put them in?" And at the end of the page, the last sentence, "We are therefore asking you for $25,000 for such and such."

Oh, finally. Just say it right up front. This is who we are, say the amount, for what project and tell me why it's important. Then the program officer thinks "Okay that does sound important, let me read on."

I think many people are worried about saying we want X in the first sentence for one of two reasons — either they consider it pushy or think it might lead to rejection.

But for reviewers it's incredibly frustrating and makes their job harder when you beat around the bush.

It's actually more polite to tell the reader what you want straight away so they can decide whether they want to use their time reading the rest of your proposal.

You're not going to persuade someone to fund a project that they aren't inclined to by forcing them to read a couple of pages of text before you get to the ask.

Funders know what they're looking for and can make pretty quick decisions about whether to keep reading. If they're not inclined to fund reading programs for eighth graders making them wait for two pages to figure out what you're after isn't going to persuade them otherwise.

Once you've captured their attention and they've decided it's worth reading, then answer the questions that floated through Sue's mind as quickly and effectively as possible.

- Do you really meet our priorities?
- Will you do what you say you will?
- Are you credible?
- Have you told me why it's important?
- Is it intriguing?

> "A great proposal writer makes the project sound interesting from the very first sentence. He or she doesn't just answer the questions or follow the guidelines; this writer engages the reader so that he or she cares about the people affected and the solution proposed."
>
> Melissa Brown
> Past Editor,
> Giving USA

Questions to Consider

1. Could my introductions be tighter?
2. Do I answer all the relevant questions and still leave a little mystery that is intriguing?

Stories Through Formatting

One of my favorite proposals was a 100+ page state grant about reading education. The RFP required a lot of formulaic material and justifications about the proposed research approach so it was dreadfully boring.

The school district that I was writing it with is in New York's Amish country and as I was driving there for a meeting I saw a sign for a quilt shop. I stopped in to look at them and realized that it was a perfect analogy for this proposal. I found pictures of beautiful quilts and began each section with a photo and description of how this part of the project was crucial to the creation of the whole quilt.

It took a comprehensive but boring piece of writing and made it engaging.

I was told that was rated in the top three in the state, so it presumably amused the reviewers enough to keep them reading, which was the point.

One of the people on my team at the district was a quilt expert and when she saw the draft told me the significance of the quilts that I had chosen for the illustrations. So, I got to learn a little more about quilts in the process too.

Element 17

Know the Dividing Line Between Critical Feedback and Writing by Committee

Illustrates GPCI Competencies

9. Ability to write a convincing case for funding

9.2. Use conventions of standard written English

Writing by committee is painful, arduous, and dis-astrous. Proposals must have one voice. Standing your ground takes finesse, but it is essential if you want to write something that sings to the reviewer's heart.

John Hicks had a couple of suggestions about how to handle situations in which groups are tempted to "help" you write.

> First of all make it clear that one person needs to be the scribe and that is you, you're going to be the scribe.

> Second, instead of giving people lots of copy to edit, give them an outline to edit, because that focuses their attention on the actual data that goes into the proposal rather than the word-smithing. Also, you will get faster turnaround working from an outline than working from narrative.

I find that it really helps put people's fears to rest when I tell the group about the success that I've had with similar grants and let them know that I really do know how to write a persuasive piece of prose.

Seek Critical Feedback

While writing by committee is disastrous, most documents are improved by critical feedback. Unfortunately, taking critical feedback isn't something that many of us do very easily.

But top grant developers have learned that curbing this tendency to go it alone can save days of work and result in a far better document.

We all assume that everyone sees the world exactly as we do, when in fact we each see the universe through our own unique lens.

Real communication occurs when we can either truly explain how we see the world to another human being or are able to view the world through their eyes.

Those magical moments of true communication can be created through writing. When we muster the grace to give our work to another person for review and accept feedback it increases the chances that we get our point across.

> "I have always found seeking out and then listening for improving arguments from colleagues helps. For all of us, criticism is difficult sometimes, so always be open to advice. Take pride in authorship yes, but listen to what other people say, too. They may spot things that seem obvious to you but haven't been expressed at all clearly."
>
> John White
> Marine Stewardship Council

It can be hard to have someone tell you that you're not making sense or that your work is boring. But it helps you to see that you are just not effectively communicating the beautiful vision inside your head and it can spur you on to find a better way.

John White told me how valuable he finds it to work in a writing team.

> I have been extremely lucky to work with a colleague who writes prose like a dream. He is an excellent, excellent drafter.
>
> His examples encourage me to think about my own style and how I can make things clearer, how I can be stimulating, how I can put arguments over in a way that are going to be convincing. We share a lot of drafts and I think that two heads are always better than one.

Not all of us are fortunate enough to work in a team like that. Mark Eiduson recommends asking someone who doesn't know your work to read it to see if it makes sense.

Alice Boyd came up with another creative solution; she trades proposal review services with a colleague in California. They are on opposite sides of the country and work in entirely different fields so they never compete.

Alice told me that being in different fields works well because they catch a lot of jargon and jumps in logic that an insider might skip over. She said that she met this person through a listserv, and that in five years they have never met nor exchanged a dime.

Questions to Consider

1. Am I confident enough to tell my team that I have the final say about editing and proposal presentation?

2. Whose writing skills do I respect? Would they be willing to give me constructive feedback on my proposal drafts or trade services?

Element 18

Seven Questions to Ask Yourself as You Write So the Reviewer Responds Positively

Illustrates GPCI Competency

4.1. Interpret grant application request for proposal (RFP) guidelines and requirements to ensure high quality responses.

A program officer once said that, "You write grants that are easy to fund and that make me understand." It's all about the reviewer and providing what they need...if I can provide a grant that's easy to fund and make their job easier, that is the way to win, so that's what I do...I try to make this as easy to follow as possible from the way I paginate, to the way I set up an addendum, to the way I provide information, to answering each question. I try to write the questions and answer underneath it so...they can see it.

Alice Boyd

All of the people I interviewed have reviewed grants at some point in their career and many mentioned how important it is; as Frank Mandley said "It will forever change you and help you understand proposal development from the reviewer's point of view."

Once you have been a reviewer you understand the environment that proposals are reviewed in.

For me, it has either been while squirreled away in a crummy hotel for a week reviewing 15+ proposals a day and never seeing daylight. Or, sitting down after working all day to review a pile of proposals before a conference call the following day while my husband was in the next room watching *House*.

Neither scenario is wont to make a person tolerant and easy going. Being a reviewer is hard work, tiring, and in many instances under- or unpaid. But it's also rewarding because you get to play a part in funding good projects and you also get to see inventive ways that people present information.

Given that top grant developers know what it's like to be on the other side of the fence, what do they do differently? We assume that the reviewer wants to fund your project.

Reviewers are looking for good projects that they feel will be properly implemented by a skilled team. I've read proposals that I thought should be funded and hunted to find places where I could give them points. But, we're also trained to read between the lines and look for the bulls*%&. In my experience, reviewers look for proposals like Alice's that are easy to fund and we don't have to struggle to award points.

So, how do top grant developers make it easy to fund? They ask themselves the following questions.

Who Are You?

When you serve as a reviewer you know that proposals are read by a broad variety of people. It's important to find out as much as possible about the reviewers.

At the state and federal level, program officers will often tell you the characteristics and skills of the people in the pool.

For foundations, the program officer may tell you about how the board reviews requests and what they are looking for. Once you know who is reviewing then you need to try to sink into their world as Johna Rodgers explained.

> I really try to picture who those three people are because I am usually doing federal grants. Who are those three people and what they are doing while they are reading? Are they cooking dinner? Are they doing laundry? Are they on their own deadline? What are they doing? How can I write succinctly and directly and leave them the trail of bread crumbs so that they can see my answer quickly and give me credit for it.

Clearly, Johna has been one of those reviewers who had her own impending deadline and reviewed proposals while tossing laundry around and standing on the sidelines of a soccer field.

Don't assume that proposals are reviewed in perfect environments by people with copious amounts of time.

What Do You Want?

A big mistake that people make when writing proposals is answering the question that you wish they had asked rather than the one that they actually asked. We usually do this because it's easier.

> "My number one job is communication. If they don't see something then it's my fault."
> Johna Rodgers
> GRREC

Sometimes, we just don't have a good answer so instead of putting the hard work into figuring out a good response, and taking the risk that we get it wrong, we tell them what we do know.

But reviewers want to know the answers to the RFP questions and its irritating to read responses that don't make sense and then have to spend time figuring out if there's anything in there worth giving points for. John White summed this up perfectly when he said,

> "What makes us successful is having an ear for what foundation officers need from us and understanding their position. I understand that they love us but they have a difficult case to make and so I ask 'how can we work together?'"
>
> Caitlin Stanton
> Global Fund for Women

What you absolutely have to do is provide funders with what they want not what you think they ought to want.

Listen to their advice about content and style. Some like regular contact, some not. If people say they want a call then give them one. Listen.

The way to contentment is to do what people ask — don't send them 30 pages when they prefer bullets. Don't annoy people.

How Can I Help You?

The grants system is an authoritative top-down system (they have the money, we don't, and we have to ask for it). However, within that structure, top grant developers relate to funders as respectful peers, and this approach is a breath of fresh air for program officers who are used to being kowtowed to or hoodwinked.

Mariann Payne said that a great grant developer is "transparent and trustworthy. Somebody who asks more questions than they have answers to."

This *"how can I help you"* approach is expressed in putting things in a layout that makes sense for them or giving them the information that they ask for.

How Do You Learn Most Easily So That I Can Explain This To You?

Not only are people unique they also learn in different ways. Your reviewer might like information in a way that differs from your preference as Frank Mandley pointed out.

> They shouldn't have to struggle to get through your proposal or to understand it. Appreciate the fact that reviewers are adult learners and will have different learning styles; some will be visual learners and others will rely on reading the printed text to acquire information.

When you write try to meet the needs of all reviewers by including concept maps and graphs for the visual learners and coherent text for others.

Am I Boring You?

Reading lots of proposals quickly is mind-numbing. Proposals all answer the same questions and after a while they all merge into one another.

To combat reviewer boredom, you can follow Gail Widner's approach, "I'm always thinking, will the reader follow this, will they follow the structure or will they be bored to death?" Make the extra effort to make your proposals memorable and stand apart from the crowd – in a good way.

> "Just make it feel personal so that the person at the other end looking at that proposal isn't thinking they are just getting a cut and paste job, that you know enough about them to speak to their interests and how this project fits their interests really, really well."
>
> Marianne Lockwood
> Orchestra of St. Lukes

Do You Feel That I Respect You As a Person and Know What Matters To You?

We all have a fundamental need to feel acknowledged and respected; it just comes with having an ego, even a nice ego.

Reviewers hate it when they feel you can't even be bothered to address them personally. Cut and paste jobs don't work because a) it makes the reviewer feel like you don't care enough about them to address them directly, and b) you don't care enough about the project to take the time to market it properly.

Of course, this may be an erroneous assumption when you know that you are working 80-hour weeks and don't have the time to tailor everything, but that's how it comes across to funders.

How Can I Simplify This For You?

The first time I served as a grant reviewer I realized to my horror that proposals that I spent weeks and months preparing are read in 10 to 20, or at the most, 30 minutes.

While it's humbling to realize that the 100+ hours that you put into a document is read so quickly, it also made me see the importance of breaking down the information into digestible chunks. Frank Mandley pointed this out in our conversation.

> Break up the text with uncluttered, easy to understand, charts, graphs and figures. And if your organization only seems to have complex charts and figures, revise them and make them easier to understand for the reviewer.

> An example is our school district's Table of Organization that is 30+ pages long and resembles a wiring diagram for the Space Shuttle — don't use it. Make your own simplified version.

Top grant developers know that their proposal might be skimmed and they have to be direct, concise, and clear. Caitlin Stanton has thought quite deeply about this issue.

> A program officer said to me "no one reads anything anymore." At a grant maker's conference a research report showed that only 50% of final reports get read...at first when I heard that, I thought "Should we even be putting so much staff time into writing? Should we just be working on the relationship building piece of this work?"

> And then I realized that people don't really read anything more, or just some of it gets read, so it means that *the writing has to be stronger.*

Instead of reading the whole thing people are picking out a paragraph here or there and *basing their judgment of the whole project on a smaller section of your work.* So everything has to be really strong because you don't know which little bit is going to get read.

But it also means you have to consider how can you present information differently.

We have been bringing *a lot more visuals into our work,* a lot more of the charts, graphics, and maps in our work.

We have seen a shift overall in society and how that applies in grant making is that it's not just about, you submit the proposal, you get the grant, you wait a year and then send the final report anymore. *We find there's a slow shift to real-time focus on reporting.* So trying to do **more mini updates** during the year especially because that kind of communication is easier for us now, rather than waiting until the end of the year loading everything into that one report that may or may not get read.

To succeed, grant developers write what will be read by their funders—not what they think they should or could write.

Questions to Consider

1. Am I thinking about the reviewer as I write?
2. What stylistic changes could I use to make my proposals more accessible for reviewers?

Element 19

Avoiding the Mistake that 70% of Budgets Contain

Illustrates GPCI Competencies

4.8. Identify effective practices for developing realistic, accurate line-item and narrative budgets and for expressing the relationship between line-items and project activities in the budget narrative.

4.10. Identify factors that limit how budgets should be written (e.g., matching requirements, supplanting issues, indirect costs, prevailing rates, performance-based fees, client fees, collective bargaining, allowable versus non-allowable costs).

As a program officer we found a number of years ago, that 70% of all budgets that were submitted to us had serious math errors in them. So from that time forward we required everybody to submit them in Excel spreadsheet format and we found that 70% of those contained errors. So we dug into them and we found that most people weren't using the formulas.

Mark Eiduson

I was astounded by what Mark told me but it makes sense that 70% would contain errors since budgets are often tweaked at the last minute when you realize that you forgot X or that Y won't be available and you need to pull it out of the budget.

However, from a funder's perspective, it just must look sloppy and jeopardize your proposal. So, if you want to win a grant, check your math and you'll already be in the top 30% of applicants.

Using the Budget as a Storytelling Device

For most grant developers, the budget and the evaluation sections are their least favorite sections to work on, probably because they are least creative. However, John Hicks has an interesting perspective that makes the budget creation process more interesting.

I learned that the principle of capital campaigns applies to foundation grant seeking. You would never do a capital campaign without procuring the largest gifts first because you have to have real working capital and you have to have a leader so that others can follow.

I think very carefully about when an organization is going out raising money to think about the sequence. Who should be asked first and for what? And why should that foundation give the amount they are giving and how does that help guarantee success?

To me it's like this whole layer of thinking you can put into a proposal that could make the proposal more competitive. It's thinking strategically about what you are asking from a foundation. What role do you want the foundation to play? Is it a leader, a follower?

I like this strategic thinking and the idea that the flow with which you seek foundation grants can be used to your advantage if it's clearly spelled out to the funder.

By using John's suggestion, you can give your budget the elements of a story, telling why you are coming to them right now and what role they are playing in the plot.

The budget can also literally give you a place to tell your story where for the narrative does not.

For example, Diane Nicholson told me, "Once I wrote a proposal to a foundation that gave us only three pages to make the case, but unlimited pages for a budget narrative. It was in writing that grant proposal that I suddenly realized that the budget really makes the case."

> "When I die nobody is going to ask for the narrative, they are all going to reach for the budget. And the reason is that's where the money is. That's all a lot of people care about."
>
> Johna Rodgers
> GRREC

Questions to Consider

1. Which colleague can I ask to check the math calculations on my budget before it goes out the door?

2. For our next big project, how could we sequence asks so that each funder relishes their role in bringing the project to fruition?

3. Do I take full advantage of the space allowed in the budget narrative to make my case?

Element 20

Five Things that Cause Writer's Block and their Antidote

Illustrates GPCI Competency

4.3. Identify work strategies for submitting high-quality proposals on time.

Grant preparation is tough work. Usually a lot is at stake, there are tight deadlines, competing priorities, and you have to make stuff up as you go along. Sound familiar? It sure is to top grant developers.

In this chapter we're going to look at the things that scare them and what they do about it; if only to give you a sense that it's all perfectly normal.

We'll see that the worry, anxiety, and apprehension that you feel in the grants development process is felt by everyone — even those who have raised hundreds of millions of dollars. The trick is to take a deep breath, focus your eyes on the prize, and not let any of it stop you from going for your dreams; which is easier said than done.

> "Know when to stop writing. If I had to pick what is the number one reason organizations don't get grants, the obvious answer is they never submit them."
>
> John Hicks
> J.C. Geever, Inc.

Shaky Project Design

When you're not clear about exactly what your team is proposing you should worry.

Red flags go up for top grant developers when they don't know enough about the project either because the details haven't been worked out or because we don't have access to the program staff. When that's the case it's hard to conceptualize the big picture and it's hard to put together a puzzle without seeing what it's going to look like.

Ann Redelfs has a nice way of handling uncertainty about the project design.

> I find it interesting that a lot of people think that they have this committee of many people and that feels, "We all know what we are doing. Everybody is in agreement because we had a meeting last Thursday." Conversations that are part of the brain-storming, "we could do this," process are much different than the written word.

> But when you have to write it down, people often respond with, *"That's not what we meant."* And they have this kind of A-ha moment of saying, *"Well, I thought that is what you said we were doing."* I love the written word because it makes people make decisions. Like we are or we are not going to do X. Whatever X is. And I love that because they do have to ultimately say yes or no to this.

Ann's way of bringing the ethereal into the tangible by writing it down helps highlight discrepancies and missing concepts so they can be addressed.

Leaving Money on the Table

Once you know what you are proposing, figuring out exactly how much to ask a particular funder for can be nerve- wracking. As John White said,

> There is always that anxiety about whether you have bid too high and so risk rejection or you have bid too low and then you think if I had asked for a bit more I might have got it. So, on the one hand you risking losing it all, on the other there's an opportunity forgone.
>
> That, I suppose, is the moment that requires both some thought and then once you have decided what you are doing any unsettling sense goes away quickly because then you have to construct the argument to justify what it is you are asking for.
>
> That is the moment of pause, the moment of thought before you start.

Lack of Communication with the Funder

You want to have a sense from the program officer that your proposal has a fighting chance. We know that sending in something cold without any feedback from the funding source isn't smart and when we are forced to do it, it can send chills down our backs knowing that we may be investing a lot of time for something that is dead upon arrival.

Dory Rand expressed this perfectly when I asked her what worried her.

> I think if it's a situation where we haven't had an opportunity to sit down face to face and really have an honest discussion: Does this meet your priorities?

Is this something that you feel positive about recommending to your board?

If you are not sure about the funder's interests or the amount of money to ask for, then it puts you in an awkward position, and I would rather have a pretty good idea upfront of how to frame the proposal and how much to ask for.

Writing Drivel

Stage fright is alive and well. Marilyn Zlotnik has raised more than $200 million and yet, "I still have stage fright before I write the first sentence. I get a knot in my stomach and I procrastinate."

Alan Tiano, who works on both tiny foundation grants and large federal grants, also owned up to it, "What bothers me? The blank page with the blinking cursor that taunts you with 'go ahead, write something, it will stink. I dare you."

Both of them overcome it in the same way, by getting started with something that's not intimidating like the personnel section or budget of a public sector grant.

Ongoing procrastination is simply a luxury that grant developers don't have, and we've learned to take a deep breath and get on with it.

I deal with procrastination by trying to just accept the way that I am. I exercise and meditate in the morning and know that I'll doodle around with little things in the morning. The heavy-duty writing will start around 1 pm and left to my own devices, will go on into the wee hours. Chastising myself for not producing pages of dollar-worthy text before noon is just self-abuse, and I try not to do it.

Years ago someone introduced me to the Emotional Freedom Technique (EFT), which is a surprisingly effective, if totally bizarre, approach. On You Tube a British guy has an EFT video on procrastination where he points out that when we procrastinate we're avoiding the feeling/outcome that we think we'll generate by doing the action.

By identifying the feared outcome we can either a) accept it or b) realize that it's not realistic.

> "You just have to stare back and start writing. It's really a metaphor for life that the brick wall that you see is just a picture of one and you just need to walk right through it and move on. Sometimes I go to the budget first or just start filling things in to get moving. Take a breath and walk forward."
>
> Alan Tiano

In grant development, putting off writing keeps us further away from failure, criticism of our work, or brutally long hours. And it also keeps me distant from success, doing good in the world, and experiencing deep joy in writing.

Faced with that, I usually plop down on the side of movement…or go get another cup of tea while I decide.

Missing Small Details

Missing tiny details is the dread of all grant developers. We all have horror stories about how missing a tiny detail cost a potential grant.

Mine is that when I first started out I was working at Cornell University and our program submitted a proposal in which we forgot one of approximately 20 signatures on one of the federal forms. Because of that it didn't even make the review process. I was devastated, but I had the world's best boss and he took it with good grace by saying they funded less than 3% of the proposals anyway and this was their way of culling the review pool.

But, I've never forgotten it and it taught me to be excessively nit-picky about details. Below are other horror stories that will make the point better than pages of my narrative.

Horror Story 1: I have learned to be a bit more of a control freak. I wrote up a public hearing legal ad and handed it to a staff person to place the ad and...she tried to condense it a bit ... to save $1.16...she left out the word 'regional' because it would make it fit in fewer lines and it cost us over $1.4 million...I have never forgotten that nor will I ever. So I proof every legal ad myself and I look at everything that goes into every grant and I do it early enough to fix it. - Alice Boyd

Horror Story 2: I submitted a proposal for funding through September 31st of the year; I learned how calendar-challenged I was (and I still am) and in addition to keeping more calendars around I always reserve time in the writing process for a proof reader/fact checker to go through the document several times to catch embarrassing gaffs like that one.

You can't be a one-man show in grant development. The funding agency actually called me to inform me it was going to fund the proposal, but for one day less than the request. When I got a little indignant as to why they were lopping off one day, I was very embarrassed to learn I had added a day to the month of September that Pope Gregory had never approved.

So somewhat humbled, I determined not to make such a silly mistake again. This happened in 1987 and I have never forgotten it! - Frank Mandley

Horror Story 3: I worked for a program that received a great deal of federal funding. We were on track to respond to an RFP that we expected, based on prior years, to come out in August and have responses due 90 days later. So I planned and paid for a family trip in July.

Well, the RFP came out earlier than it had in prior years, and guess what, key parts of the process occurred in July. However, I wasn't in touch with the program officer in the federal department, so this all snuck up on me. My boss ended up having to do the proposal — and boy, was she mad.

I learned to work more closely with federal program staff, to call monthly or so to check in, and to watch deadlines and releases scrupulously. - Melissa Brown

Horror Story 4: I had a proposal returned to us ...because I had the Chief Operating Officer's (COO) signature instead of the Chief Executive Officer's (CEO) signature.

You can build good relationships and have a good proposal but it can all fall apart if you miss the deadline or get a COO signature instead of a CEO signature. - Caitlin Stanton

It's very, very hard to come to terms with the fact that people have lost their jobs or that elderly people won't have access to meals because we missed a detail.

I think that many of us have felt that gut-twisting pang when we have to acknowledge that our mistake took a toll on our community. So we now err on the side of extreme caution.

All of the consultants talked about how they have learned not to leave things until the last day. This was not the case for staff members, probably because they have less influence over the work flow than consultants.

One final note about paying attention to details. John White mentioned the power of being an organization that consistently meets deadlines and pays attention to details.

> Don't miss deadlines, be they deadlines for submitting proposal or for submitting reports and the latter is equally important. Once you have a grant, servicing that grant is very important.

> You will appear very sloppy if you do miss deadlines and I think what you want to cultivate is a positive image, as an efficient organization that is worth supporting and not a problem one that the funder always has to come back to ask for things.

When you are preparing grant proposals while simultaneously running an agency, you're not going to be able to do a perfect job. Your client's needs will make demands on your time that require you to make choices.

Hopefully, this chapter will help you clarify which things you can let slide and which things to prioritize— conceptualizing the proposed project and triple-checking the small details.

And when you find yourself putting off the writing, know that you are in good company and just buckle down and do it anyway.

Questions to Consider

1. What circumstances cause me to procrastinate or freeze when I'm preparing grants?

2. Who could I recruit to help me get unstuck when I get stuck? Consider telling a friend or colleague about when and how you procrastinate and ask them to be your go-to person when you see yourself falling into that pattern. Even knowing that you've told on yourself and that you have a person to reach out to will make a difference.

THE SECRETS

Element 21

Honor Your Power

Illustrates GPCI Competency

6.2. Identify circumstances that mislead stakeholders, have an appearance of impropriety, profit stakeholders other than the intended beneficiaries, and appear self-serving.

So far we've looked at what top grant developers do and how they do it. I haven't talked about what they don't do.

During the interviews it was obvious that there a few things that you'd never catch a top grant developer doing and being falsely humble is at the top of the list.

Don't Whine and Beg

A question that lies at the back of all grant developer's minds is, "How desperate do we have to appear to get the money?" Some organizations ask for grant funding when they don't really need it. For example, large institutions sometimes construct new buildings with their own endowment and then seek grant funding to pay for it.

On the other hand, you don't want to give off an air of desperation that diminishes the funder's trust in your capacity to deliver on your promises.

Walking this fine line can be tricky. However, top grant developers are crystal clear about where the line is and on which side of it they stand. As Frank Mandley said,

> I realized it was important to view yourself as an applicant, not a supplicant, for grant funds. Too many grant applicants take a posture of more or less "begging" a sponsor for funds in their proposals... They seem to confuse addressing a need or problem with appearing needy themselves.

> I don't think humility sells a proposal and I've never been good at it anyway.

The push to use the "needy button" doesn't just come from within nonprofits though. As one person said "whining appears to be encouraged and rewarded by some foundations-they ask 'what keeps you up at night?' We are encouraged to talk about the hard life that we lead and I won't engage in it."

Foundations do this for a good reason. They consider that their investment is a drop in the bucket compared to a) the need and b) government funding and so they really want to make a targeted investment where it's needed most. But asking the "How much do you need us?" question creates a victim attitude among a lot of nonprofits. It's clear that top grant developers don't do victimhood or begging.

But why not? To many people it seems to make sense that the more that you need the money the more foundations and government reviewers should want to support you.

There are three main reasons that top grant developers don't do it. First, it's annoying, and as Johna Rodgers so eloquently points out,

> I wish I had a dollar for every time I read someone else's proposal and they talk about poor pitiful me because of the budget cuts we can no longer do this. Yes, you can. Somebody somewhere made a decision on how to spend money and they made a decision

not to spend it on your thing. Poor, pitiful you. It isn't the reader's fault.

Don't make them listen to it. They have their own problems.

The second reason: it's just plain ineffective, as Alan Tiano explained,

> Some grant developers make it sound like the end of the world is coming if they don't get this money…I think it shows a dysfunction.
>
> You wonder, does the organization really think this? If they do then they are just too dysfunctional to receive money.
>
> That shows an organization that is in panic mode and has a management style that reacts rather than thinking things through. That they don't have a Plan B. It shows an immaturity of an organization and their management.
>
> Generally you come across that with small organizations that have founder's syndrome. They just don't have an overall perspective where their service fits into the continuum. They tend not to collaborate well with other organizations, which we know creates a lot more efficiencies in the system. It tells me a lot.

It's human nature to want to back the winning horse or at least the gutsy one that's coming up fast against all odds.

Most of us don't want to be associated with the one that keeps stumbling and getting injured despite the best stabling and training or the loser that just doesn't have what it takes to win. Grant funding is like that too.

Funders want to be associated with the champions — whether they are the best and strongest nonprofits in the field or the one that has all the smarts and pluck to pull it off if you just give them a helpful nudge. So, whining about your 10 straight losses is the last thing that you want to do.

The third reason that top grant developers don't whine is that it's fallacious. One top grant developer explained this very well.

> Foundations ask, "What will you do if you can't raise the money?," and the truthful response is that we'll do it anyway. We'll trim the budget, we'll get the money from someone else...if it's worth doing, then we'll do it.

And he continued to put his finger on an inherent problem within the system. He said,

> If a foundation asks "What if we gave you money for something that you couldn't do otherwise, what would it be?" The answer to that question is "something frivolous and extravagant." The thing that I'll only do if you give me this money, is something that is less than essential.

> I think herein lies the tension between the foundations' need for impact and our organizational needs for creation.

The Alternative to Whining

So, if whining is annoying, ineffective, and fundamentally untrue, what approach do top grant developers take?

They come from a place of self-assurance and clarity of purpose that Frank Mandley captured as telling the funder, "I've got a solution for the problem you are interested in and I can deliver the goods!" It's not simply a "have I got a car for you, pretty lady" spiel but is undergirded by a solid belief that we have a great product.

So, if you're tempted to seek sympathy for your dire fiscal situation—don't.

Instead, show that you're an agency that's in a tough spot due to circumstances beyond your control, but that you have the vision and passion to work your way out of it.

> "Come at if from a 'we are so great at doing what we do that we are going to go out and do more of it. Our cup is always full. We have our happy hat on, we are the experts and we are going to bring this service to our district because they need it.'
>
> Johna Rodgers
> GRREC

Don't Be Too Humble

Grant developers may be humble beasts, but they aren't shy about selling their organization. Spend a little time at a Grant Professionals Association Conference and you'll find yourself surrounded by strong-willed, opinionated, and smart people.

As Mariann Payne says, "Don't shy away from demonstrating your organization's power in this area. Be bolder and brassier than you are comfortable with."

If you're unwilling to enjoy selling your organization or project, then you're not well suited to the job.

Questions to Consider

1. Am I willing to brazenly brag about my organization and our projects?

2. Do I always pitch my organization as one that is strong and headed in the right direction or do I lapse into "woe is me" on occasion?

Element 22

Be Impeccable with the Truth

Illustrates GPCI Competencies

6.4. Distinguish between truthful and untruthful, and accurate and inaccurate representations in grant development, including research and writing.

6.8. Identify unethical and illegal expenditures in a budget.

You can't tell a lie in an application. Look at your data sources and pull out those data that support you.

Don't give them everything. Go through and find those honest facts about your organization that you can put the best spin on and maybe that's where you put a little varnish on with how you say things, but never tell a lie.

Frank Mandley

At one point, all grant developers have been asked to lie. Time and money are the two biggest pressures in our society and grant developers deal constantly with both demands. It's almost inevitable when money and jobs are at stake and time is added into the mix that we'll be asked to do things that are expedient but we know aren't right.

It's easy to lie in an application, and there's a decent chance that you might not get caught. So, being in a position where you're under pressure to lie and you can do it without too much difficulty almost demands that grant developers have a clear sense of ethics — or face the specter of sleepless nights. Nancy Withbroe talked about this.

> I think with foundation work you can be fudging the numbers on the budget, and you can be asked to fudge the timeline.

> You're the one in the end and you have to think about the relationship with the donor and the ethical principles you want to uphold, and make a decision about how you are going to handle that situation. You need to educate the people who are doing this, probably more out of ignorance than out of malice, and how to work through that can be really tricky.

Nancy puts her finger on the crux of the matter here. People who ask us to cut corners often don't realize that what they're asking is either illegal or unethical and once you explain it they're happy to let it drop.

Successful fundraising is dependent on building and maintaining solid long-term relationships and those simply can't thrive in an atmosphere of deceit.

We've all been in a position where we had to take a stand on something. This is Frank's story.

> The first time we did a mini-grant competition, a project my boss wanted funded didn't get funded. So, she said, "What are you going to do about this?" I said, "Well, if you ask me to fund them in even though their score didn't warrant it, you will get that with my letter of resignation." She said "Well, why don't we do this. Why don't we move the bar lower, and fund everybody down to them."

> Well, I could live with that ethically but I couldn't say let's take these people who scored 50 and the cut was 60 and put them in the funding category because you like them.

The biggest temptations to cover things up come after a grant is awarded.

Projects often don't progress according to plan. For example, the person that you need to hire has to undergo new background checks and can't be put on the payroll until six months into the grant. Sometimes these things just come up and sometimes it's because we made a mistake in our planning.

How we handle them is a test of our ethics. It's tempting and pretty easy to cover up small mistakes but as Bill Smith said, "little mistakes can kick up dust so try to deal with your mistakes honestly." Doing so isn't only expedient but helps nurture long-term relationships that are crucial to our craft as John White points out.

> Don't hide things — be upfront. Explain it and the consequences and suggest how you want to remedy things... If you don't and you run into trouble you simply lose credibility and ultimately if you lose credibility you're not going to get a follow-up grant down the line.
>
> It's long-term funding relationships that matter and are extremely valuable. So be upfront if there is an issue...and in my experience most funders are only too understanding that there are delays.
>
> But there's no advantage in pulling the wool over people's eyes.

The other thing that keeps grant developers honest is being in a community that has a standard of ethics.

Nancy Withbroe told me "a really good grant developer has thought those things through and is a member of an organization that has an ethical code and really upholds that."

> "I think you have to use integrity when you are varnishing the truth and know you are not varnishing the truth... I am a firm believer that you can take something rough and make it smooth and really sell it. But there is that moral line that you have to really think about and I chose to live my life on the white side of gray. You just have to draw that line for yourself."
>
> Alice Boyd
> Bailey Boyd Associates

If you aren't part of an organization such as the Grant Professionals Association or the Association of Fundraising Professionals then you are less likely to have had conversations with fellow grant seekers about potential ethical dilemmas and how to handle them.

Attending meetings where these thorny issues can be aired in a safe environment gives grant developers the leg up when they come face to face with them.

You Can't Polish a Turd

Grant developers are as skilled at varnishing the truth as used car salesmen. We know that you can focus on a car's low mileage and downplay the occasional rust spot.

But, we have to know when we are shining a gem or, as Frank Mandley said, polishing a turd.

> You can't polish a turd. When you get done there is nothing left. I heard that from the Dean of the College of Education the first day of a new job when he said, "I'm sorry I wasn't here to greet you on your first day but we had a Council of Deans meeting. It went on a long time because we were trying to

polish a turd and we discovered that after three hours you can't."

Top grant developers have developed the capacity to tell the difference between varnishing the truth and polishing a turd.

Distinguishing between the two is a matter of discernment and personal ethics. I draw that line by putting myself in the funder's position. If it's a public sector grant I think about how hard I worked last year to pay my taxes and whether I want my money to be spent on this project or not.

If it's a foundation proposal I ask myself if I could ask my parents to support this project with a clear conscience.

Another way of keeping on the right side of the truth is taking Frank Mandley's and Alice Boyd's approach, which is to assume that they are public documents that will be published in the newspaper.

Sometimes, we just need to get our hands dirty and directly address ugly situations.

Alice Boyd told me about a project she worked on that required her full reserves of integrity and finesse. Her client had been in a highly publicized scandal because of the actions of one bad employee and her challenge was to "portray the agency as strong, humbled by the experience, but much wiser and very capable." They called community leaders and explained the situation and asked for their suggestions about how to move forward. She told me,

> We really were able to gain some consensus from community leaders that what we did was very valuable and then we were able to present that with the backing of all these people.
>
> This had been front page in the papers, and I addressed it directly in the narrative. I talked about what had happened with the agency and how it had

really catapulted them into some very introspective work.

So we were able to really take a very negative thing and bring in the credibility of community leaders who worked with us.

Interestingly, Alice told me this story when I asked her about her best work. While it's a cliché, our biggest challenges also give us the greatest opportunities for experiencing our strengths.

Turn into a Pretzel

The biggest trap is turning yourself into a pretzel. That has always backfired for us.

Marianne Lockwood

There's always a little dance between funder and grantee as we try to fit our projects to their priorities. As Nancy Withbroe frames it,

Most grants are restricted, like it or not, that that just is the way the grant makers are, so how do you find the grants that are restricted in a way that still is appropriate for what you as an organization want to do and what the people that you are serving need and simultaneously, not overly restrict it so much that you don't have any money to keep the lights on or to pay the support staff? It's a dance that we all play and it's all too easy to turn yourself inside out and become a pretzel.

There are several flavors of pretzelizing and none of them are nutritious. First is to pursue funding for something that you're not fired up about. As Jonathan Bank says

> I have wasted a lot of time writing proposals for projects that I would do if they were funded but was not committed to doing regardless of the funding.
>
> I learned that it has to be worth doing. You need to decide what you want to do and then get funding for it. I think that maybe sometimes professional development people have learned to cultivate vagueness because their executive director doesn't know what he wants, and they are trying to leave him enough room to figure it out later. I know that those proposals don't get funded so I don't even bother.

It's easy to see why they don't get funded. The passion isn't there and the funder will pick it up in a nanosecond.

Projects have to be propelled by some form of energy whether it's passionate love or its alter ego, anger and frustration. When someone is moved to act for the sake of the collective good then that project is likely be funded.

Questions to Consider

1. Am I really clear about where my ethical boundaries are and do I feel comfortable defending them? If not, seek guidance from the local chapter of the Grant Professionals Association or Association of Fundraising Professionals.
2. Do I know where our boundaries are for creating programs that align with our mission or are we a little too willing to "pretzelize" ourselves for funding?

3. Under what circumstances is our organization ever tempted to cross over the grey line? Have a frank conversation with your team about when that has, or could, occur and ask what you can point in place to avoid it in the future.

"Don't take an existing program and give it a new name and try to sell it as something new. It's putting a new cover on an old book and funders can smell it a mile away… if you don't have all the pieces and you start creating things out of air to compensate to respond to a question, the grant reviewers pick up on that instantaneously."

Diane Gedeon-Martin
The Write Source Inc.

Element 23

If All Else Fails, Shop for Cowgirl Boots

I usually hear through the grapevine that awards are being announced so I wait, full of hope and trepidation, for the phone to ring...like a teenager waiting for a boy to call. I carry my phone everywhere and check e-mails relentlessly. The knot in my stomach starts growing and I question my intuition when the phone doesn't ring. Even after 21 years in business, on the occasion that we're not funded, I feel sick. Did we forget something? Did we mess up?

Alice Boyd

Are top grant developers immune to the sinking feeling that I get when the proposal is turned down? Or is it just me?

I found out that it hurts us all. Responses to my question about rejection ranged from "crawl under a desk and hide" to "badly, I wallow in it for day or so."

By far the most honest and interesting response was Mariann Payne's.

I actually think it's really hard, because one in three efforts succeed and you spend so much time and you say "The next time I spend this much time I am going to shop it to three places." Never done that. It's just very hard. I shop for shoes when I lose a battle like that. I handle failure by eating and going shopping. Lots of shoes have been palliative and curative. After losing a National Endowment for the Humanities grant last year, I went shoe shopping and got a very beautiful pair of red cowgirl boots, and I just feel better when I put them on.

The concept of palliative shoes will live on with me for years to come. But people with thin skins don't last long in our business and experience is a good salve.

After being in the business for a long time you see that sometimes truly excellent proposals don't get funded.

For foundations, it might be that the stock market crashed and while they love you and your project, they can't fund it right now.

In the government discretionary process politics and personalities can get in the way. Some review processes are more transparent and unbiased than others but it's sometimes not a competition based purely on merit as Frank Mandley pointed out,

> I have always felt that a competent government grant developer can control only about 50% of the competitive grant process and that the remaining 50% is a matter of chance, e.g., which rater is the proposal assigned to?; what are the rater's biases?; have the raters been oriented and trained by the funder to be a reviewer?; does the rater have a firm grounding of the purpose of the grant program?; or does the rater have a background or expertise in the field...which the proposal addresses?
>
> You can try to prepare for these in the preparation of the proposal, but you really can't control them.

When you have seen excellent proposals get turned down for spurious reasons you learn to take rejection with a grain of salt.

"A friend who is in sales says 'some will, some won't. Get over it and move on... Hearing no is part of our job and you can't connect your self-worth to it.'

Mark Eiduson
Flintridge Center

The Measured Response–the Debrief

After the initial pang of rejection fades and the crush of defeat eases, top grant developers look squarely at the detritus for what we can learn for the future.

For government grant developers this takes the form of asking for the reviewer's comments. Frank Mandley talked about what his team learned from doing this.

> Sometimes this exercise was very informative and other times it was not. We often got ideas about how we could present some information in a clearer or more compelling manner and tried to learn some lesson to include in future proposals.

> Sometimes your biggest flops are your best learning experiences. On other occasions, it was obvious from the raters' scores and comments that the rater was absolutely clueless and/or did not take the review process very seriously.

Some foundations and corporate funders don't give any feedback and so you're left in the dark about why it wasn't funded.

One of our interviewees pointed out that this is a deliberate decision because it invites a response. If they say "We didn't fund you because of X," then non-profits will argue the point and foundations just don't want to go through that process.

> "One of my mantras is that many grants begin with the word no."
> John Hicks
> J.C. Geever Inc.

Nevertheless, top grant developers always try to get feedback anyway and use it as a way to develop the relationship and understand the funder more completely.

Start with the assumption that this is another stage of the relationship building process rather than that you have done something wrong. John Hicks explained that he approaches these calls by first recognizing what's true.

> What program officers can't control is how that committee and how that board is feeling about how much money are they going to distribute, and what their priorities are, and what is the emotional response to the committee to the project and to the organization.

> There are some intangibles that you can't resolve until the rubber meets the road.

Accepting the capriciousness of the process, it allows him to approach the debrief as an exploration without judgment.

> First of all, it helps to find whether we are 3mm apart or 3 miles apart. It's that response that can inform a second approach and the approach can simply be a matter of timing, it could be a matter of "we would like to see some clarification because our board wants to feel more comfortable about topic A, or topic B."

> Sometimes the board is intrigued with the organization. They don't want to support the project but they may want to support something else the organization does.

You can hear in this quote an absence of judgment. There is no hint of "you should have said yes, what's wrong with you that you didn't understand our request or what's wrong with me that you don't want to fund us."

The genuine question for John is, "Please tell me about your point of view and are there ways that we can come closer together?"

Resolve

Oh, I never take no for an answer, never, never. As far as I'm concerned no means come back later and it has worked. Yes, occasionally there have been times when the no has really meant no and I hope I am sort of sensitive enough to realize I should stop banging my head against that particular brick wall. For the most part I have been pleasantly surprised by waiting a bit, maybe taking a different angle, seeing if there's another way to get in the door. Is there a different contact? And going back.

Marianne Lockwood

In this business you need tenacity and a willingness to embody Winston Churchill's definition of success: "Success is the ability to go from one failure to another with no loss of enthusiasm." Marianne certainly appears to embody that sentiment and the result is that she recently raised $25 million for her organization.

Perseverance also comes from experience. I was once told by an NSF program officer, "Well, you've only applied once. You shouldn't have expected to be funded. We usually don't fund before the third try."

Ann Redelfs has probably heard similar things from program officers and gave this advice,

When something fails I think people have a tendency to give up and that is usually not the way any foundation or government agency wants you to behave.

They want you to try again. That is why they give you feedback. What I find unfortunate is when somebody has an unsuccessful proposal and they just give up and a year later they are still saying to themselves, 'Well, we tried submitting this proposal but we failed so we are not going to do that again.' And to me that's a real tragedy. Even with the same idea, try it again, and focus on how well you match with the granting agency's requirements.

Just figure out a way to make it different, find a new partner, angle it differently but learn from that and move forward instead of giving up.

Redefining Failure

When I asked people "How do you react when your proposals fails?" a lot of people immediately questioned what I meant by failure. Several people distinguished between a proposal being rejected and it being a failure. For example,

It's not a failure when it's a good proposal for a good project that is the result of good planning—that can always be reused. I don't get invested in the money but more in developing good planning—because grants are no use if they are bungled. - Gail Widner

I do not count a proposal as a failure if I crafted it with excellence. Some projects are a hard sell, sometimes we simply cannot get the information we need to strengthen the proposal, and some funders have their own ideas and priorities. If what I send out the door shines of excellence, then it's my own private success. If I send a proposal out that I'm not proud of, and that proposal is funded, then I am inwardly dissatisfied, even if my agency is happy. - Bill Smith

Failure to me would be we had it, but we blew it because we forgot something or we blew the site visit. Rejection isn't that. - Tony Silbert

What I heard in all of these responses were altruistic individuals who are genuinely disappointed when a proposal is rejected.

But, they also haven't identified themselves with success and if they know that they helped conceptualize something worthwhile then they can be satisfied at one level...and then go out and buy cowgirl boots to soothe the other part of their personality.

They also have a natural persistence and willingness to try again despite setbacks, knowing that they can't control every aspect of the game. If you have faced the sting of rejection and given up on some funders, you might want to reconsider, look carefully at what you could have done differently and learn from the experience, and then try again.

As Billie Jean King said, "For me, losing a tennis match isn't failure, its research."

Questions to Consider

1. How do I handle rejection?
2. Can I use past rejections as conversation starters with funders?
3. Do I consistently look for what can be learned from each loss and then build that into my grant development strategy or do I run away and never look at it again?

Element 24

The Art

The art is in the attention to which his or her audience reads her grants — like how an audience watches a play.

Jonathan Bank

Grant development is both an art and a skill. The skill lies in learning, practicing, and eventually internalizing the elements described in this book. But there is also artistry.

Just like love flourishes more easily when there are strong boundaries in place, grant artistry emerges when the fundamental skills structure is in place. In love, the stronger the bonds of trust the more secure the boundaries containing the relationship become, the more our loving, vulnerable, compassionate self can show up without threat.

And likewise, when you have mastered the 23 elements of grant development already covered in this book, the basic structure is intact, and there is space for synchronicity and the magical 24th element to emerge.

What do I mean by artistry? Every top grant developer knows the sheer joy of being in flow when you look at the clock and realize that you've been writing for five hours when it feels like five minutes. Or, the meeting where you just know that you've hit on the right idea or just recruited the right person to complete the team.

It is a space imbibed with ease, power, and clarity in which words effortlessly flow through you onto the page or into the meeting. Of course, those times are precious, but they are the moments that we live for.

The incredibly frustrating thing about being a writer is that it's nigh impossible to force the flow state into existence. We all know that it strikes when it strikes and not until it's ready. For me, it often happens when I'm distracted and taking a break such as walking my dog or taking a shower.

I think that grant developers have an advantage over others who have less intense deadlines. Since grant development is by necessity, intensely focused work, it forces a level of absorption that often triggers these moments of inspiration.

But, as I found when writing this book, when there is no pressure of a deadline it is tempting to sit around, muse and wait for inspiration to strike and then cry in frustration when it does not. So, grant deadlines, like almost everything else, are a mixed blessing.

But I think there is another level of artistry that we don't talk about.

But since this book is intended to expand the conversation about gifts in our field, I will share that my two strongest gifts are that of writer and medium. So, I will take another leap and talk about the role that my psychic gifts play in my work to good effect.

We have long been told that there is the physical world and the spiritual realms. But it is my belief that everything we see is the living embodiment of spirit—including grant developers.

We have all experienced the power of synchronicity—knowing who is calling on the phone or having a long lost friend call hours after you have been thinking about her.

I believe that everyone has the capacity to connect to the eternal one to some extent. For me, the connection seems to be stronger and more easily accessed than for other people and becomes stronger the older I get, as I believe is the case for many women.

It is my experience that we communicate energetically at sub-atomic levels through our thoughts and feelings. It is as if we are walking radio transmitters and receivers. Scientists tell us that the left brain is the rational and logical and the right brain is creative and intuitive. And by intuitive we mean connected to the spiritual realms.

Some people argue that it is our right brain that is communicating with the eternal one. I'm content to let the research scientists continue that investigation and I'll read the results with interest.

But, what I know from personal experience is how tapping into our unseen interconnectedness can have practical everyday benefits for grant developers. Here are a couple of examples.

I was hired to work on a project with a large organization's senior leadership. I was a little nervous about the project and so before our first meeting, I meditated and my guidance told me that the project was about creating a place of safety for the community that didn't exist. It didn't make too much sense given the type of project that it was so I took it with a grain of salt.

A few hours later, I turned up to the meeting and sat next to the CEO. Half an hour into the meeting she turned to me and said "Jane, do you know what this project is about? It's really about creating a place of safety for our community that doesn't currently exist." I was floored but I also knew that it was a deep vein of truth and my job was to portray it in a way that clearly resonated. I did exactly that and the $8 million project was ultimately funded.

A year later, an Executive Director whom I admire called me and said the State had released an RFP that they were in a really good position to win and it was due in 10 days, would I help? As much as I loved the organization, I am no fool so I gave him a point blank, no.

However, he happens to be born charmer and visionary and he explained that he would focus his entire team's energy on the project, I would have access to everything that

I needed, that they could even draft some of the sections, and they just needed my expertise to put it all together. Then he told me what it was for and how well positioned they were to win. Softened, I agreed.

It was one of the most fun and rewarding experiences of my career. As promised, their entire team pulled together to help me and the ED called me each evening to cheer me on and see what I needed.

Regardless, it's still nigh impossible to put together a state grant in 10 days, but everything fell into place. Ordinarily I would spend a week working on a needs statement—in this instance I had one day. When I sat down at the computer to start the research, within half an hour I found a newly released scholarly study that was exactly what we needed to support our case. The entire project flowed like that.

One thing after another fell into place. I knew that it would get funded and it did, for $4 million. Indeed we were the highest scoring project in the field. That project was clearly aligned with the higher good and fell into place accordingly when our team tuned into that.

The worst experience of my career was something else entirely and came just a few weeks later. I was hired to work with a large coalition to submit a massive federal proposal. The team was very nice and competent, and I had no doubt it could be done in the time that we had. We had lots of meetings but nothing seemed to go right.

It was just one thing after another. We switched approaches midway through, people disappeared on vacation without telling me, including the person who hired me (lesson learned: ask about vacation schedules at the beginning of projects), and even my computer died three days before submission.

The process was like pulling teeth and I was miserable. When we finally submitted the proposal, the person who hired me told me that he hadn't really wanted to do the project but his agency had the funding to hire me and other people had talked him into doing it.

Needless to say, it didn't get funded and I'm glad. I can't believe that the team would have worked together any more effectively with a few million dollars in their pocket than they did during the development process.

Coincidentally, I worked on these two projects within weeks of one another so I could see that it was not likely that I was the determining factor in how the projects had gone.

Those two experiences were in such stark contrast that it led me into years of intensive soul searching about what I do and how I do it.

I have come to believe that projects have their own energetic integrity and when we honor that our work flows. I also know that grant developers can be channels for manifesting our collective consciousness.

In hindsight, I realize that for decades I have been using my psychic senses in grant development without being conscious of it.

For the last few years, I have been building and refining my mediumship skills and I now consciously use them during grant development. Sometimes, it is in subtle ways in what occurs to me as deep listening to my team. At other times, I actively seek guidance from the ethereal.

I do not believe that I am alone in relating to our work in this way, it's just that many of us do it unconsciously or choose to keep it quiet.

In these two quotes, I can hear that Alice and Marilyn are instinctively tapping into what will connect reviewer and grantee and the energy surrounding a project.

I think the artistry is in making the reviewer feel your pain or your enthusiasm. If you can make a reviewer tear up you have done your job. If you can make a reviewer feel compelled to really advocate and get it funded, you have done your job. There is an art in writing a proposal that is authentic, sincere and compelling. - Alice Boyd

You need truth and heart. Truth is speaking plainly, clearly, and directly about the ideas and strive for those qualities. Heart is trying to make sure that the energy I have cultivated through intensive planning process. It's knowing their goals and vision so that when I write about it that energy comes through in the writing. The difference is that one sings and another just sits on the page. - Marilyn Zlotnik

My daily practice is to begin the day with an hour of meditation. I started out with just 10 minutes but quickly saw that when I take the time to center myself, I am exponentially more productive than when I let myself be pulled in five directions. So, over time I've increased the length and depth of my mediation and not only I am more productive but things just seem to fall into place — the right piece of data shows up, someone helps out and does something in half an hour that would have taken me three, etc.

I hope that this chapter will resonate with some people and stimulate discussion about the intersection of the physical and spiritual in our professional field.

Questions to Consider

1. Which projects feel like swimming upstream? What is fundamentally missing in those projects that that if it were present would make a difference?

2. Is there a habit or practice that I know benefits my productivity in the long run that I don't make time for? What would it take to put that in place for a month?
3. In what circumstances do I feel free to do my best work? How can I create those circumstances around me now?
4. If you supervise other grant developers, I encourage you to ask them how you can support them to have their work be more fulfilling, creative, and satisfying.

The Big Picture

I invite you to take a few moments to review the 24 elements I've outlined in the book and assess your strengths and weaknesses. Check the elements that you think could be stronger for you or your organization.

RESEARCH	
1: Three Core Beliefs About Prospect Research	
2: Knowing When to Respond to a Request for Proposals	
BUILDING RELATIONSHIPS	
3: Know Each Person's Role and Responsibility in Foundations	
4: Getting Through the Door	
5: The "Getting to Know You" Process	
6: Finding and Empowering Your Champion in the Board Room	
7: Four Ways to Respect Your Funders	
8: Why You Should Always Contact Government Program Officers	
PROGRAM AND PROJECT DESIGN	
9: Getting Your Team Thinking	
10: Promise Only What You Can Deliver	
11: The Art of Eliciting Information from Very, Very, Very Busy People	

12: Government Grant Developers' Dominatrix Gene	
13: Three Ways to Nurture Strong Collaborations	
MAKING A CASE AND WRITING THE APPLICATION	
14: The Power of Story: Writing a Bodice-Ripping Romance	
15: Mastering the Art of Persuasion	
16: Be Crystal Clear	
17: Know the Dividing Line Between Critical Feedback and Writing By Committee	
18: Seven Questions to Ask Yourself as You Write So the Reviewer Responds Positively	
19: Avoiding the Mistake that 70% of Budgets Contain	
20: Five Things that Cause Writer's Block and Their Antidote	
THE SECRETS	
21: Honor Your Power	
22: Be Impeccable with the Truth	
23: If All Else Fails, Shop for Cowgirl Boots	
24: The Art	

I invite you to go back and re-read those elements and consider what you can do to build proficiency so that you have access to all the links in the grant development chain and can take a holistic approach to the process.

Heart-Centered Grant Development

I have developed a unique approach to grant development training that I call Heart-Centered Grant Development.

It is the marriage of technical skills and spiritual concepts in pursuit of personal, organizational, and community growth. Just like this book, it is based on a holistic approach that recognizes our interconnection. It is grounded on 10 core concepts and beliefs:

Interconnection: This approach honors our interconnection and gives us strategies for tapping into its power.

Intentionality: While projects have their own essence we are not simply passive actors. The way that we approach each project has impact. Whether we own them or not, we bring to our work conscious and subconscious beliefs, attitudes and suppositions that impact us, the people we work with, and the outcome. The energy with which we plan a project and write shines through in the document whether we acknowledge it or not.

Gratitude: Identifying each person, organization, and community's strengths is the basis of gratitude for what you bring to each proposal.

Sufficiency: Our culture trains us to believe that there is not enough and that we are not enough. We examine this assumption and its impact on our grant development work.

Dreaming: Power lies in envisioning the world in a new way and has the clarity and perseverance to align our actions with that vision to make it real.

Spaciousness for Creativity: Grant development is a linear and high pressure business. We are all about getting from point A to point Z progressing through predictable steps along the way. But the world isn't a linear place. Just look at a maple tree or a stream or a crocus. There's very little that is linear and uniform about them. There is power in slowing down, taking the dog for a walk in the midst of the mayhem, going around in circles a few times and seeing what emerges.

Truthful Communication: It takes courage to tell the truth, especially when it's less than palatable but it sits at the heart of grant development.

Action: Without action everything is just a dream. Or, as Arnold Glasgow said, "Ideas not coupled with action never become bigger than the brain cells they occupied."

Courage: Taking bold action in the face or your own or others' doubts can bring up fears. But we can learn to act even in the face of doubt or fear and be courageous.

The miraculous: Love, beauty, and grace are the intangible threads that make our world glisten. They are present in every work of art, act of kindness or courageous stand.

When we consciously do grant development work it becomes deeply rewarding sacred service. If you would like more information about our classes based on this approach and the elements in this book please visit www.grantschampion.com

ABOUT THE AUTHOR

Jana Jane Hexter, GPC, President of Grants Champion, has written well over 150 successful proposals and raised more than $28 million for her clients in the last few years alone. Her clients include school districts, higher education institutions, and human service agencies throughout the U.S.

Born and raised in England, she graduated from Cornell University where she was a Ford Foundation Clusters Scholar. She is a captivating teacher. She has spoken at the Grant Professionals Association and AFP National Conferences. Her "Presentation on Presentation" at the National GPA conference was given the highest ranking by conference attendees. She taught grant writing at New York University's George H. Heyman Jr. Center for Philanthropy and Fundraising.

She served on the National Board of Grant Professionals Association and is a former chapter board member of the Association of Fundraising Professionals Finger Lakes. She also served as a Subject Matter Expert for the Grant Professionals Certification Institute (GPCI) to develop the Grant Professionals Certificate exam. In addition, she has served on peer review panels for New York State and the United States Department of Education.

Jana is also a medium and channels with the spirit world. She leads spiritual circles as another form of healing work. She is exploring ways of integrating her vocational and spiritual gifts.

She lives in Ithaca, NY, and loves to hike in the beautiful state parks near her home and swim in the lakes during summer, and whiz down ski slopes a little too fast in winter. Best of all, she likes to hang out with her two kids and black lab—a little dark chocolate and purpose-filled work makes it all the sweeter.

You may contact her through www.grantschampion.com

The fruit of Silence is Prayer
The fruit of Prayer is Faith
The fruit of Faith is Love
The fruit of Love is Service
The fruit of Service is Peace

Mother Theresa

Made in the USA
Lexington, KY
22 February 2013